P9-EDF-287

Managing Information Security:

A Program for the Electronic Information Age

Managing Information Security:

A Program for the Electronic Information Age

James A. Schweitzer

To the ASIS Information Resource Center — with best wishes and appreciation!

Jim Schweitzer

3/10/88

BUTTERWORTH (PUBLISHERS), INC.
Boston   London

Library of Congress Cataloging in Publication Data

Schweitzer, James A., 1929-
    Managing information security.

    Bibliography: p.
    Includes index.
        1. Computers—Access control.   2. Electronic data processing depart-
ments—Security measures. I. Title.
QA76.9.A25S36   658.4'78   81-17063
ISBN 0-409-95055-6   AACR2

Published by Butterworth (Publishers) Inc.
10 Tower Office Park
Woburn, MA 01801

Printed in the United States of America

To Ray Humphrey and Brian Hollstein, whose encouragement and faith sustained my efforts in putting this book together. And to Henry Wold, who provided invaluable review.

CONTENTS

PREFACE

Security managers have long been concerned with the protection of business assets — plant, inventory, personnel. The "electronic information" age developing in the 1970s and 1980s has increased the scope of this concern to include perhaps the most valued asset of all — information.

This book describes the reasoning and activities which created an electronic information security program for a large international business. This is not a technical treatise for computer experts; there are many excellent works available on "logical" security and encryption. Nor is it an instruction on physical security measures. Most security managers already are knowledgeable in this area. Rather, it is a philosophical exposition on the thought processes and activities involved at not inconsiderable cost, in instituting an electronic information security program. This was done in the context of an overall information security effort.

This book differs from most "computer security" texts in that it addresses a *total* information protection scheme — recognizing that protecting computers in data centers is only a small part of the activity called "electronic information security." The total program envisions the computer-using activities as definable groups, and attempts to speak to these groups in tailored fashion — recognizing the differences in approach and outlook among managers, scientists, secretaries, engineers, and professional data processors.

This book is about a program structure. The program described is an attempt to deal with the new "computer age" information security requirements. To that end the program suggests some tested approaches:

1. The computing activities in a large company are viewed from the prospect of service users.
2. The "personal computing" phenomenon is given special attention.
3. The total information processing environment is covered, including office computing.
4. A comprehensive program structure, founded on authoritative management support, is outlined, with examples.

It is my hope that security directors will find this book helpful in structuring their thinking about the electronic information explosion and its security implications. Computer security people should find this book a means of comparing courses of action (and, perhaps, disagreeing with those of the author). The procedures and structures discussed here have proven to be effective in developing a security program that deals with electronic information in its entirety. I offer this material to the reader as a model by which other programs may be created to meet the security needs brought on by the coming of our ''Electronic Age.''

1
BASICS OF
BUSINESS SECURITY

To ensure a common starting point for considering the development of a security program for electronic information, a brief review of traditional business security functions is in order.

For most companies, security consists of physical, information, and government security activities. The first two are concerned with conserving business assets; the third, with complying with government requirements when so demanded by contract.

Government Security

Developed in current forms during World War II, this activity ensures that businesses comply with employee clearance and information protection requirements of contract and law. It is only indirectly related to the subject of this book.

Physical Security

This function provides for the protection of people, facilities, and other physical assets from threats of disorder, theft, or destruction. It applies to, and uses, electronic systems. The importance of physical security continues into the electronic information age. In most cases, this is the most mature, fully developed function in a business security department.

Information Security

This function provides for evaluation, identification, and protection of business information, which is one of a business's most important assets. Traditionally, this activity dealt with concerns for security of information in paper or oral forms. The arrival of the computer, with its electronic form of information, changed these concerns significantly.

DEFINITIONS

Some terms are used which may not be familiar to the security executive. Among these are *electronic information:* any information or data processed, stored, or communicated by use of a computer or electronic system. *Operating system:* the executive system or intelligence system, provided by the computer manufacturer as a program, which causes the computer to react to command or instructions. *Logical security:* those security measures implemented through programs written for that purpose, and loaded into a computer. These security elements may also be implemented through hardware, designed by engineering methods and delivered as part of the computer circuitry. An example would be a password identification system. Other definitions are found in Exhibit 3.3.

MOTIVATION

The use of computers in all phases of business activities and reports of misuse of computer systems for illegal or damaging purposes are cause for increasing concern for the security of business information. Although a formal program, such as that suggested in this book, may be implemented, a prerequisite to effective security is motivation of people.

Real security for electronic information does not result from rules on pieces of paper, assignments of people, hardware facilities, or software systems. Security occurs if and when, a majority of employees agree with the need for a security effort and consent to the means selected for protection. In the end, the effectiveness of all controls depends on people's being willing to comply. Consent to a course of action, especially among an intelligent and technically astute group of people, implies understanding of goals and agreement with selected means.

Successful security indoctrination will explain the rationale for information protection and will achieve employee agreement with that need. Further, a business must develop understanding and acceptance of the rules and procedures. To those ends, security indoctrination should

1. describe the value of information, its use in the product development and marketing processes, and the legal implications of information security should litigation occur;
2. explain alternatives for protection and the reasoning for selection of certain methods;
3. describe the information valuation system (Chapter 1) and offer illustrations of its application;
4. show the concentric levels of protection (Chapter 3) and explain the content of each level, demonstrating uses for the various valuations and mentioning published security standards.
5. define procedures for handling, marking, and transmitting information in physical (document) or electronic form;
6. explain special concerns where electronic processing devices are in use, especially those systems common to the particular operating unit, and specify protective measures; and
7. emphasize that meticulous personal observation of the rules is essential to continued business operation.

The electronic information security program must be the result of decisions made at the highest decision level. Managers throughout the organization are expected to support and enforce security requirements. Employee perception of management concern for security will have much greater effect on actual protection than mere publication of rules. Certain actions will reinforce the importance of security:

1. Tell employees about their unit security coordinator (Chapter 2) and his/her function.
2. Have regular area security checks performed by the security coordinator and by the unit security function. Use a form to report violations in a well-thought-out manner. Increase pressure as the majority of people begin to comply.
3. Ask managers to mention security measures and requirements in their regular staff meetings. (Some of our most successful companies do this as a routine matter.)
4. Give special attention to motivating the security coordinators, providing them with instructions, materials, and a sense of importance.

People respond when the motivation and climate are right. Creating the proper motivation requires an analysis of the unit environment and a recognition that security is not an end in itself, but a necessary support to business operations.

A particularly heinous crime always brings calls for better law enforcement, which later die away as other matters press on the conscience of citizens. Similarly, concerns for business security readily become forgotten until some incident occurs. Motivation contains more than a bit of fear, and an effective security function provides the right amount of monitoring and measuring:

1. The audit function should include a security module in every audit performed.
2. The corporate manager provides security reviews on request and performs security surveys at major installations.
3. Operating unit security managers are encouraged to do security reviews as means of analyzing vulnerabilities and identifying corrective actions.
4. Security elements for computing systems should be used to the fullest extent practicable to reduce risk and to assist in prudent management of information resources.

Morale or attitude is not the responsibility of the security manager, but it is one of his/her concerns. Especially in a high-technology group, the attitudes and feelings of people toward the company are critical. Opportunities for mischief abound and cases of employees striking out at employers through computing systems or equipment are not unusual. Security managers should work through the personnel function and line managers to monitor employee attitudes. Observance of employee job performance may provide evidence of developing troubles.

Security means that management is controlling the valuable resources of a business. Security procedures can provide the catalyst for management attention to needed controls. Productivity and management effectiveness can be improved through proper application of security. In one case, monitoring of terminal users' activities for security purposes led to management discovery of wasted computer resources and unnecessary spending. In another case, installation of encryption systems required use of multiplexers, which resulted in savings in the cost of communications circuits. Demonstration of management benefits from good security helps convince employees (and management!) that effective security is a contributor to profitable business.

Effective security measures also benefit the employee. Many business people caught in improper and illegal acts are, on the surface, good employees. They are upwardly mobile, and have ambition, drive, and good social relationships. They work harder and longer hours than average. The conclusion is that they did not start out as criminals or miscreants. Rather, the embezzler or attacker tends to be an employee with technical talent who (a) has a financial problem; (b) is too proud to ask for help; (c) knows how to cheat or is able to break through the system controls; and (d) can overcome conscience by rationalizing.[1]

Effective security systems help avoid losing good employees and help employees resist temptation by making (c) too risky and (d) too difficult. A strong deterrent to improper action is attained by getting someone else involved. Setting up security systems requiring collusion among employees is a primary protection. Active security functions make employees aware of the risks in attempting a theft or computer penetration. In organizations where security is not taken seriously, employees may feel that "everyone's doing it" and may be encouraged to attempt various illegal or improper acts. Some people apprehended in the course of a crime have cited the lack of organizational interest and care as a reason for their actions!

THE VALUE OF INFORMATION

Business information is an asset. Significant costs are incurred in developing, processing, and communicating information. Certain kinds of information, such as the results of research and engineering work, may be of strategic value. Other pieces of information may be potentially damaging to a business if exposed, such as a decision concerning replacement of a key executive. Without going into a tedious listing of the various types of information and their relative values, suffice it to say that information may have value like any other asset, and hence should be protected.

Information Valuation

Once while riding on a train, a fellow passenger told me that he was in the grocery wholesale business, and that he and his colleagues needed no information security program because "in the grocery business there are no secrets." One cannot argue the point without better information than that available to the writer, but it is questionable whether the management of that particular grocery firm would agree that there are no secrets.

Almost every business has information it wants to keep "private." (Personnel records, at minimum, require protection.) The first step to developing and proposing a program for the protection of business information is the evaluation of that information. This evaluation or "classifying" of information provides a value factor for each piece of data.

This value factor may represent any or several of the following risks:

- damage to the business if the information is made public;
- financial loss if information is changed improperly;
- business cost if the information is destroyed;
- competitive effect on the business if the information comes into the hands of a rival;
- legal vulnerability if information protected by law is improperly released.

The established information value factor is usually represented by selected terminology such as "Secret," "Private," "High Value," "Restricted," "Confidential," "Proprietary," and "Personal." The particular terminology selected is unimportant, but there must be a structured meaning which reflects levels of value (and hence, levels of protective effort). For example, information evaluation might be expressed in this structure:

Type	*Title*	*Value*
Highest value	Secret	Information which, if released to unauthorized persons, would likely cause grave harm to the business
Middle value	Proprietary	Information of important competitive value
Protected information	Business use only	Information which, by its nature, would be embarrassing or would represent loss of privacy if divulged

Most businesses will want a special value factor to cover personnel records, because of the legal exposures in handling personal data. One such value factor might be:

Type	*Title*	*Value*
Personnel information	Personal	Personal information which a reasonable person would wish restricted to specified, authorized employees only.

The value factor structure is the bedrock for all programs of information security, including a program for computer-processed information security. Careful evaluation of the information used in the business is an absolute requirement in assuring business continuity.

Value factor decisions must be made on a company-wide basis, and at an authority level which can act across organizational boundaries. Procedure for marking and protection must extend to all information producers and users. The activities suggested herein are a part of an overall business effort, and should be viewed in that context.

Information identified as having significant value must be protected in all forms in which it occurs. This means that a program which protects computer-generated outputs but disregards manually prepared reports and memos is of little consequence. It is not the computer itself which is of concern, but rather the information processed. (The computer is one of many physical assets used in business, and the protection of such assets is important but outside the scope of this text, which deals with a program for protecting electronic information.

The valuation of information and the resulting assignment of value factor identification, or classification, are the first basic requirement for establishing a program of electronic information security. Although risk analysis may, in some limited cases, provide guidance for required protections, in most cases, effective security in terms of cost and results depends on accurate identification of information value factors. (Chapter 4 discusses uses of risk analysis and the alternative use of value factors.)

2
THE NEW REQUIREMENT

It is said that more books are published now yearly than were published in the entire history of mankind before 1950. A large portion of this expanding knowledge is in technology. And a good part of this technology has to do with computing. Almost every advance in computing technology is of interest, and a challenge for business managers responsible for protecting information assets.

Technology in the form of applied computing has added a new requirement to the traditional functions of business security. This fourth function, called electronic information security, interfaces with the traditional business security functions but has new dimensions and special requirements. This chapter describes the technology, its use in business, and the security concerns arising from electronic information processing.

WHY THE ELECTRONIC INFORMATION REVOLUTION?

The effectiveness of operating a business may be measured in terms of efficiency and cost. Efficiency relates to how well a task is done in relation to business goals. Cost is a measure of the resources consumed in completing a task.

The goal of management is to increase profits by increasing efficiency through decreasing costs, for a given task. In almost every case, increasing efficiency (decreasing costs) requires investment. The net effect of investments to improve efficiency and/or reduce unit costs is called "productivity."

Economics and Investment

Productivity in the United States has decreased from an annual rate of $+3.4$ percent in the years 1946–1950 to a rate of -2.6 percent in 1980.[2] This sorry state of affairs reflects the weak incentives for investment, the result of political decisions and taxation. But some of the loss in productivity must be traced to transfers of large portions of the work force from farming and manufacturing to the service and administration areas.

Investment in productivity outside manufacturing and agriculture has been very weak, comparatively. Capital investment for each manufacturing worker during the period 1969–1979 averaged $24,000 while investment per office worker in the same period was only $3,000. As might be expected, productivity increases in manufacturing far outpaced those of the office, by 84 percent to 3 percent.[3]

The large numbers of people moving from traditional work sources to administrative and service work tend to pull down overall productivity. The office is the worst case example. People in offices are performing administrative tasks in ways very similar to those of fifty or even one hundred years ago. Communications, paper creation and handling, and information storage and retrieval have changed little since the invention of the telephone. One positive factor is the xerographic copier, which allows distribution (communication) of paper in parallel.

Integration of functions is still a long way off. With over 50 percent of the work force currently termed "knowledge workers," business is forced to address low productivity in this group, which is an important factor acting as a brake on efficiency and profits. ("Knowledge workers" are people whose activities deal with information, such as managers, professionals, and secretaries.)

TECHNOLOGY

A turnaround of the worsening productivity trend requires that business provide tools to make employees in all parts of the business more effective. The most promising tools for this purpose are those systems and mechanisms which apply computing technology. Examples of such systems are industrial robots, information systems for on-site support of marketing people, and office automation systems. The latter two examples represent technology developments which are changing the ways businesses handle information. These changes directly affect the concerns of security managers for business information. And these changes, which are coming faster each year, are the result of some key developments in computing technology. These developments have allowed increasing scale of circuit integration using silicon crystals. Since thousands of tiny elements can be batch manufactured (with the connections costing only one-hundredth as much as wire), the circuits are very cheap. The number of components per chip has doubled every year since 1960, so that in 1980 over 150,000 components can be interconnected on very large scale integrated (VLSI) chips which are one-tenth as big as a postage stamp. VLSI has attributes which make it ideal for the placement of computing power in all kinds of machines — washers, typewriters, robots, telephones, automobiles, tiny calculators. These attributes are:[4]

1. economy, with the cost of a logic gate decreasing from $2 to $4 in 1970 to $.003 to $.005 in 1980;
2. reliability, in that the mean time to failure of VLSI components is 100,000 times better than that of computer parts in 1955;
3. small size, with 64,000-bit chips of a size which can be imbedded in telephone receivers;
4. energy efficiency resulting in less power use and fewer problems with parasitic circuits;
5. capabilities for dealing with the microscopic world. The production of miniature circuits depends on other miniature circuits to control production processes.

The results of research and engineering of computers and their component structures have been threefold.

First, computing power has become unbelievably cheap, in terms of 1955 values and relative inflation of other goods and services. The cost of processing, in inflated dollars, has decreased about 25 percent per year. Since wage costs have been increasing at a slightly higher rate over the same period, there is great economic motivation to invest in computing systems which replace human effort.

Second, the efficiency of computer hardware and its servicing software has improved remarkably. During the late 1970s, operations per second doubled about every two years. A recent product advertises a speed of 800 million operations per second, and large memory access time will soon be at the rate of 10 million per second. These speeds make very large data base processing attractive and provide a base for extended distributed processing networks which use a central data store for reference and large file processes.

Last, solid state technology has provided continuing miniaturization of computing circuits. The "credit card calculator" is an everyday example. Not only has the size of general purpose computers shrunk, but miniature components allow computer intelligence to be imbedded in all kinds of devices including automobile fuel and braking systems, home appliances, telephones, and copiers. See Table 2.1 for further technological developments and the security problems which accompany these advances.

SECURITY RULES IN THE INFORMATION AGE

Security thinking has remained behind the leading edge of technology application. During the 1960s and 1970s a security "gap" developed. That is, infor-

Table 2.1

COMPUTING TECHNOLOGY AND SECURITY

Technology will deliver	Evidenced by	Having the effect of	With these results	Causing these security concerns
Higher computing needs	IBM H series (1980) with speed four times IBM 3033 (1978). CYBER 205 with 800 mil. operators per second. Large memory access time down from 200 nsec in 1980 to 100 nsec in 1985	Increasing volume of activity at central processor sites for economic reasons	Time-sharing in some situations such as scientific work. Very large data base processors	Centralized high-volume data banks require more effective logical access controls. Unauthorized access is potentially more damaging in this case.
Higher density data storage	New magnetic disk or videodisk permanent storage with capacity of 1 trillion bits (equal to 2900 tape reels)	Increasing volume of data at central sites in data bases for efficiency reasons	Very large data bases	Theft or misuse of media could result in serious loss or compromise of information
Reduced costs per instruction processed	At rate of 25 to 30% annually, from $2 per mil. instructions processed in 1977 to $.67 in 1980	Wage costs drive business to replace labor intensive tasks	Computing moves to local sites. Personal computing as stand-alone or distributed system	Distribution of computing power to personal level implies individual acceptance of responsibility for information protection

Table 2.1 continued

COMPUTING TECHNOLOGY AND SECURITY

Technology will deliver	Evidenced by	Having the effect of	With these results	Causing these security concerns
Lower memory costs.	In 1980 MOS memory cost is 50 millicents per bit, to decrease to 15 millicents in 1985.	More use of memory as temporary storage. Larger processors.	Very large central processors.	Same as above and below.
Continuing miniaturization	Power delivered on a fixed size chip doubling each year.	Computers (some software loaded) appear in mundane devices, and as labor replacements in offices, homes.	Imbedded processors in office and home devices. Personal computing.	
Flexible and economical networking	Functionality and data format independence, via imbedded microprocessors. Coaxial cable at 6 mil. bits/sec. being replaced by fibre optics at 45 mil. bits/sec. Voice digitizing offers data/voice combination efficiencies.	General use of message handling services, remote computing, time-sharing, etc. first in business then in homes.	Distributing of information. Storage, processing, and retrieval capabilities.	Capability to access information through networks means that an effective system of access management is required.

mation security planners failed to grasp the importance of the development of computers in terms of safeguarding information. Security efforts remained largely physical in nature, while information took on nonphysical forms such as electronically generated digital or analog signals.

Business has always consisted largely of exchanges of information and goods (with modern banking, the transfer of funds is also an information transfer). Information has traditionally been transferred via paper or word of mouth. The equipment and tasks in the traditional office represent developments from paper-handling systems. In/out boxes, file cabinets, mail deliveries, envelopes, posting clerks, typists, and desks are all developments in support of paper-oriented business systems.

Security of information, then, has depended on physical protection features which serve paper creation and handling operations. Such features include marking and stamping, enveloping, file cabinet locks and strengthening, restrictions on distribution of papers, and document covers and logs. In the office of the 1920s, paper handling systems were remarkably similar to those in use today. The telephone is probably the only significant change in business procedure up until the development of the plain paper copier in the 1950s.

Computing technology began to affect business operations in the early 1960s. Initially a replacement for routine posting, computing, and transfer operations (such as customer billing), computer systems soon began to be used for generating decision information, such as management reports and summaries.

Management concentration in the early days of computing was on replacement of labor-intensive functions and on control of the high cost of computer hardware. The unusually high values represented by early computing equipment resulted in concern over the security of the data processing site. Attention naturally focused on facilities, environment, and physical protection. The computer, to the security manager, was merely another critical and expensive piece of equipment — much like the equipment in the laboratory. As such, it received the usual protections from unauthorized physical access, fire, etc.

The computer, however, was not merely another piece of expensive equipment. It was a revolution in the way information would be handled. Of course, only a few computing scientists and professional science prognosticators foresaw this.

Management's general perception of the true nature of computing and its related technology explosion was slow in coming. Unfortunately, the security community lagged behind management's perceptions by ten years. While systems and industrial engineering were busily applying computing to process control, work-in-process reporting, inventory control, laboratory experiments, etc., security continued to regard the world as paper oriented.

Security application of computing and electronics, except for the military and high-quality national police work (such as that of the FBI), developed concurrently with miniaturization. Recognition of the changing information protection situation occurred, prior to 1970, only in special situations (such as some IBM publications on data centers). The security community, therefore, finds itself in a catch-up position. Computing science is putting electronic information systems in place, down to the personal level. This revolution has profound implications for the business security manager, as follows.

Information in electronic form has qualities which are novel and startling.

1. Electronic information is not limited by physical distances. That is, such information can be delivered to a person or place tens of thousands of miles away with virtually no lapse of time.
2. Electronic information access does not require physical presence or the provision of some particular device. Anyone with access to a telephone can obtain information. There is no need to visit an office or unlock a cabinet.
3. Transactions against electronic information files can be invisible, even to the computer. People or machines can see, change, destroy or remove information without leaving a trace, physical or logical (i.e., electronically recorded).
4. Enormous volumes of electronic-form information can be contained on a small disk, tape, or cartridge. Per item 3, information can be copied on a tape or disk at lighting speeds without leaving evidence that such copying has occurred.

It should be noted that the transition from manual to automated systems is a gradual process. Some fairly important business functions have already been fully converted (for example, payroll processing), while others are only in very early stages (such as message processing or "electronic mail").

The electronic information security program is in a broad sense an effort to keep protective measures abreast of technology. Success in this effort and a measurement of how well we succeed require an understanding of technological advances. Further, the security implications of technological innovations and developments must be known, suitable protective measures identified, and reasonable implementation means provided.

Every technological change has a potential security implication, if only because the technology deals with the process of servicing information needs. Every time an information service is provided, a potential vulnerability is created. Such vulnerabilities may be in information transfers, storage, retrievals, or processing (computing). A potential vulnerability exists because every movement or change of form of information provides an access.

Businesses must determine whether such access creates a risk, and if so what protective measures must be provided. The application of computers in business presents characteristics which are keys to new security vulnerabilities. Among the characteristics of advancing computing uses are:

1. Continuing operation of centralized computing activities (data centers). There are also smaller centers which use one or more mini-computers as central file stores and network hubs.
2. Rapid growth of time-sharing, including the use of vendor services (computers, software, and networks). In some cases, time-sharing services (terminal connection to a central processor where files and computing power are shared with others) are intermingled at the data center with batch processing (i.e., files are used for both purposes).
3. Information is transmitted over multiple networks. From both economic and security viewpoints, this is an unfortunate situation, because costs and vulnerabilities increase when technically different networks interface.
4. Critical information (highest value factor) is transmitted over many lines, processed, and stored in many places.
5. Distributed computing is providing terminals which can do local processing and file storage concurrently with capabilities to send and retrieve information to and from central sites or other local stations.
6. Personal computing, especially in offices, research, and engineering, provides knowledge workers with desk-top capabilities to generate new information, compute, send messages, process text, create graphics, etc.
7. Office computing, a primitive form of personal computing, allows the secretary to do word processing, text processing, communications, and image transmission.

Consideration of the developing use of computing may lead to the conclusion that traditional data processing and the newer office systems are converging. That is, since both use electronic information forms and both offer communications, intersystem movement of data is a logical development. Some recently announced systems offer integral data processing/office services packages, while others provide interfaces for computing or word/text processing packages.

In considering the security implications of computing technology development, however, it is best to ignore such "convergence" concepts. By viewing office automation (in personal computing and other forms, such as word processing) as a portion of the total computing technology development, it is simpler to identify the key security concerns. This is because the primary change in the general computing environment, caused by technological innovation, has to do with communications. In essence, the increasing ease of transmission of computer-processed information allows the extension of computing activity outside the "data processing" area, to the personal level at employees' work stations and eventually to anywhere a telephone line is available. Security concerns resulting from information technology applications center around this primary change.

The development and delivery of distributed forms of computing, where local terminals connected to a network allow withdrawal and processing of information, present a real challenge to security managers. Not only do we face continuing threats to the traditional data center environments, but we now have information, much of it in decision form (of strategic value), turning up in hundreds of offices and other places where vigorous security measures, like those in a data center, are unrealistic.

Figure 2.1 displays the overall computing systems array with vulnerabilities.

Information may be transferred electronically across a state or across a continent in the blink of an eye. This capability makes computing science extremely valuable and important to business (and governments), but it also changes, in a drastic way, traditional security requirements. From the communications power of computing technology a first rule of information security may be postulated:

First Rule of Information Security

Control of access to information requires both physical and logical controls. When information is evaluated and found to have a sensitivity which demands protection, certain requirements must be established having to do with (a) the right to have the information and (b) control of capability to access the information. The second part, that of controlling capability to access, has to do with limiting who can see or have the information.

Capability to access, in the computerized business environment, means:

1. Identification of authorized information users. This may be done by a formal list, by job assignment, by department function, by personnel characteristics, or by any set of descriptives which allows a basis for exclusion of those not authorized.
2. Provision of access capability to those authorized. Access may be provided by inclusion on a mailing list, by giving a combination to a safe, or by providing passwords for logical access controls. It should be carefully noted that logical access controls require three elements to achieve acceptable protection. These elements are (a) identification of the accessor, or his/her claim to be a certain person; (b)

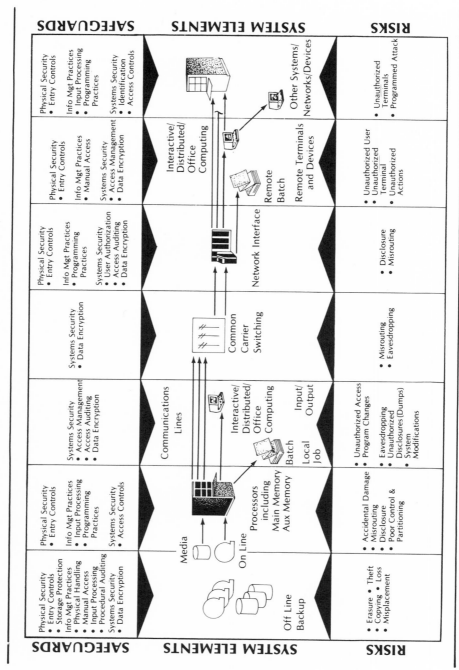

Figure 2.1. Computing systems vulnerabilities. (Adapted from U.S. Department of Commerce, NSB.)

authentication of the claim by means of something known, something owned (such as an ID card), or something inherent (such as a fingerprint); and (c) authorization, whereby the system matches the authenticated accessor against a preset authority to see or do something.

The first rule of information security means that, for protection purposes, information must be assumed to exist in both physical and logical (electronic) form, and that the electronic form has no physical location constraints. It can appear anywhere! Good security systems will insure that it can appear only where and when proper authority exists for its appearance.

Since transactions against an electronically written file leave no visible trace, a second rule of information security can be developed. This second rule relates directly to the rules of evidence used in law. Access to information traditionally required either oral contact, where one person "spills the beans" to another, or physical contact with a paper, file, cabinet, or office. These things leave traces or clues, such as human observations, fingerprints, pry marks, breaking, etc. Logical access leaves none of these.

Second Rule of Information Security

Computer systems containing sensitive information must provide records of all accesses and must be resistant to attack. Access records on computer systems are similar to the usual "sign-in" when a stranger enters a facility. They are not protection, but only history. The access control method described under rule one may be effective, but the method, in itself, may not be resistant to skilled attack. Such resistance is known as the "work factor." The penetration work factor (PWF) refers to the effort an unauthorized penetrator must make to access the information successfully. Just as a burglar who finds that a house is secured may go to easier pickings, the computer penetrator may be discouraged and go to another target!

Resistance to attack means a significant PWF. Since it must be assumed that the would-be penetrator has technical competence, the PWF must be of considerable cleverness and robustness. A suitable PWF might contain these elements:

1.   Authorization tables which limit access for authenticated individuals to narrow slices of the information bank. Usually, this means that the successful penetrator will have to discover other passwords, phone numbers, codes, etc. for each further bit of information.
2.   Operating systems which are resistant to penetration. Work has been done by Honeywell and others on a secure system, and is still under-

way. In the interim, the work factor is enhanced by severe limiting of access to high level (privileged) codes, storage of all passwords in encrypted form, the use of transforms (handshaking) instead of passwords to access control files, and automatic terminations when improper passwords or invalid access attempts are made.[5]

3. Providing multiple defenses through which an attacker must progress. For example, access to an operating system can be restricted to certain terminals, which may then be physically placed in restricted areas. This would form a first line of defense with the logical access controls being the secondary line, and encrypted files the third line.

4. Encrypting high-value information whenever it travels across communications circuits. Accessing in-transit information is relatively simple and cheap. Any public utility communications system must be considered to be insecure.

Current technology developments indicate that encryption circuits implemented on chips will be available, at reasonable cost ($200 per unit?), in the near future. At this writing, a link implementation of encryption costs about $3,500. Eventually, information system products with encryption options, perhaps field-installable, will be available.

Encryption must always be end point to end point, and should never require decryption/encryption at an intermediate point. (See Chapter 3 for a more complete description of encryption and uses.)

Considering the gold mine of information contained in the millions of tapes and disks in use, practical measures are needed to provide the same measure of protection as offered for documents. All magnetic media should be stored in containers with strength equivalent to that provided documents of the same classification. High-value factor information must be encrypted when stored on magnetic media. Further, controls and inventory methods should provide assurance that all media are available and accounted for at all times. Thus the third rule:

Third Rule of Information Security

Effective controls and storage systems must be provided for all magnetic media (tapes, disks, etc.). These new vulnerabilities and resulting security requirements bring the conclusion that the traditional security structure cannot deal with the challenge. Further, even if the structure is changed and the necessary competence levels provided, an after-the-fact program will not do the job. Protection must be built into systems and hardware. These are the new security requirements. As we shall see later, security depends on (a) proper elements being provided in developing information processing systems and (b) security managers ensuring that hardware products put into use contain necessary protective features.

Some years ago the National Association of Security Dealers opened a new major data processing center. The center's employees, reacting to the security surrounding the plant, named the site "Fort Nasdaq." (This data center had all the available physical security features, approaching a military level of protection.) With today's distribution of computing to the personal level, such a "bunker" approach no longer suffices. Information security necessarily depends not only on physical security but more importantly on measures which recognize the general spread and availability of electronic information. Ergo:

Fourth Rule of Electronic Information Security

In addition to the logical and physical security elements in previous "rules," *the security program must have as a primary goal the indoctrination of all employees as to the responsibilities inherent in the use of electronic information processing systems.* Employees must be willing and capable to recognize information which should be protected, and to take necessary action to obtain classification and provide resulting protective measures. This is much different from knowing the rules to follow when a piece of information is already classified. Automated information systems may create novel information of great value...when produced it will have no markings or signs. The employee must make value judgments immediately.

Technology is providing computing and communications power at the personal level, deliverable wherever telephone connections exist. This means that the security of information, now deliverable by electronic systems at any place or time, must rely on individual awareness and actions. Personal responsiveness to information security rules and procedures will come about only if an effective training and motivation program is provided. The usual training of selected people will not suffice, but must include all "knowledge workers" (defined earlier). There will be training involved as the new information processing systems are put into place. This training provides opportunity for inserting a module on electronic information security.

The new technologies offer not only improved information processing and communications, but in themselves the technologies offer better information security. This will not come about automatically, however, for in installing and using the new systems without considering security, new and more dangerous vulnerabilities may be created. Applying the new technology in secure ways means using the electronic system capabilities to enhance security.

This can happen only when system users are aware of the potentials and demand sophisticated security subsystems when the hardware is selected and/or the system is designed.

PROGRAM PEOPLE

An effective security program for electronic information cannot be achieved through pieces of paper and telephone calls. People must be in place at operating sites to initiate, monitor, assist, and review program activities.

The program we are describing envisions two levels of effort: at the corporate level, a manager of electronic security, and at the operating units, electronic security coordinators.

The manager of electronic security is the senior advisor to corporate management on electronic security technology matters. He develops and monitors program effectiveness, and reports to the corporate director of security. He should have significant experience in information systems development and operations, and a general competence in business management. Job descriptions and an organizational chart are provided in Exhibit 2.1 and Figure 2.2.

Below the manager of electronic security, forming a network throughout the operating units, are the electronic information security coordinators (or security coordinators). The security coordinators act jointly and singularly to identify, develop, and install suitable protective elements for their units. Security coordinators are appointed by operating unit or division management, typically from the information systems activity, although in some units the security coordinator might best be an electrical engineer or someone of similar background.

The corporate program announcement and policy serve as authority for the manager of electronic security to request appointments of security coordinators (see Exhibit 3.1, page 34, for examples). Security coordinator assignments may be full- or part-time depending on unit size, scope of computer use and systems development, size of data center, or similar criteria.

The security coordinators must be trained by the security manager. If the proper people have been selected, as per the job requirements statement, this training amounts to a motivational explanation of the scope and purposes of the policy and the program. Throughout the implementation and ongoing operation of the program, the security coordinators will serve as the program lifeline. Their eventual contributions to both the unit-level and overall business electronic information security effort will far outshine the efforts of the security manager. The security coordinators will, if motivated, develop innovative methods suitable to business needs in a far more effective fashion than can the security manager from his central (and distant?) position on high. His role

MANAGER, ELECTRONIC SECURITY

Responsible for monitoring and encouraging operating division compliance with policies concerning business security. Through appointed divisional security representatives,

1. develops and publishes security standards;
2. reviews divisional operating plans for compliance with standards;
3. coordinates the development and proposal of new security standards responding to business and technology developments;
4. advises and assists division managements in implementing effective security programs;
5. advises and reports regularly to corporate management on progress toward meeting policy.

SECURITY COORDINATOR

Responsible to division management for the development, implementation, and maintenance of a Digital Information Security Program meeting corporate policy requirements. Through appropriate division line managers,

1. monitors development and installation of required digital information security elements;
2. develops division plans for implementing and maintaining full compliance with corporate policy;
3. reports periodically as required to the corporate security manager on progress and problems;
4. participates in the development, coordination, and publication of security standards implementing policy;
5. assists local managers, where necessary, in the development of procedure in support of standards.

Exhibit 2.1. Job descriptions

should be that of offering guidance and coordination of the security coordinators' efforts and innovations.

INTEGRATING THE NEW FUNCTION

With the advent of the "information age," the age of computing, most large businesses find themselves with two security functions. Although both have the stated intent of conserving company assets and resources, differences are

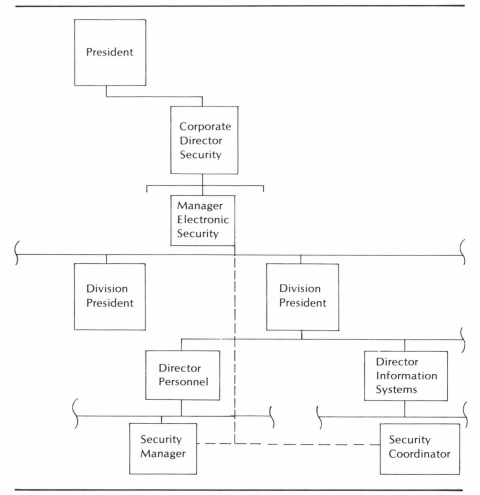

Figure 2.2. Organization chart.

notable. The traditional security function involves responsibility for guarding the physical and information resources of the business. Typically, this function is aligned organizationally with Facilities or Premises Departments. The function is usually managed by an employee who is a long-term member of the Facilities Department, or a retired police or military person. The new "electronic security" function has responsibility for protection of the business's information processing resources, including a major portion of the time-sensitive information used (and processed, therefore, by computer). Usually, this function is aligned with the Information Systems Department and is managed by a computer specialist.

The problems which result from this dichotomy are not publicized but are evident to anyone who has worked on security problems in a large business. Evidence of the difficulties are found in many examples, to wit:

- Senior management often thinks of security people as being in the same group with maintenance, cleaners, and chauffeurs. Professionalism and technology are not credited to security, although surely those attributes are present in a company of any size.
  RESULT: Security and computer people deal with management at different levels.

- Computer people tend to speak in "computerese," leading to common charges of trying to confuse the layman. Security people respond similarly.
  RESULT: Security people either comply with electronic security requirements blindly or put up resistance because of poor communication and understanding.

Computer security people have a different view of risks and protections, resulting from currency with, and understanding of, the information explosion. Facilities security people are usually dealing with the physical world only.
RESULT: While the computer security manager may be trying to protect information in electronic form and also the resulting printed outputs, the physical security manager may have no requirement for document protection. The same information generated on a computer may appear elsewhere in manually typed form, totally exposed.

Physical security methods have acquired a considerable infusion of technology. Minicomputers are used in many applications. Unfortunately, these applications are seldom coordinated with computer staffs, resulting in duplication, waste, and confusion.
RESULT: An area control system uses employee job description codes to determine who may be granted access. These codes are also found in the employee master records maintained on a computer. The security people, however, laboriously enter employee authorizations manually from listings. The computer security people use a tape dump to update a similar file used in terminal control processes. As might be expected, the physical access file is frequently "out of synch."

Physical security requirements can be counterproductive when the security staff does not comprehend computer processing requirements.
RESULT: Compartmentalization of a large data center for security purposes destroys the smooth functioning of production processes.

These examples are not meant to imply that both the computer security people and the physical security people intend to do a poor job. Just the reverse: in the face of dedicated, purposeful staffs, the missed opportunities and problems are prima facie evidence of poor communication. The resultant misunderstandings create a barrier to the cooperation and common purpose required if a business is to achieve an acceptable level of protection.

Towards Achieving Unity and Accomplishment

The people engaged in protection of computer-processed information and those responsible for physical security should have a clearly defined statement on their responsibilities and relationships. An examination of the tasks of these groups shows that there are a surprising number of interfaces. The functions are mutually dependent. Two important examples:

1. Information must be protected wherever it appears, in any form. Physical security measures must protect the physical representations of information, while electronic security measures must protect information in computer-processing forms (usually digital signals). In some cases, the protective measures from each type are alternatives — as when a terminal might be protected by either (a) providing a locked facility or (b) establishing an access control system through the use of security software (passwording, etc.).
2. Physical protection (the outermost layer of the protective structure) depends on robust physical measures. Whatever the technical facilities provided, one wishes to keep unauthorized persons away from the computing equipment, communications wires, etc. Physical security thus becomes essential to protecting computer-processed information.

An unambiguous statement and understanding of the responsibilities and mutually supporting relationships among physical security and technical security staffs will establish the need for understanding. Generally, the key to achieving good working relationships is the familiarization of physical security staff with computing technology.

The electronic security coordinator should act as technical advisor to the physical security manager and staff. The advisory process works both ways, as when the electronic security coordinator needs help in the designing of processing or office facilities. An effective relationship between physical and technical security people depends on (a) common understanding or purpose and goals (which for information security must be clear and crisply defined, especially as to information valuation, marking, and protection across all forms); (b) regular meetings to discuss programs and problems (no room here for secret agendas); (c) technical training for the physical security staff (since more and more physical security uses minicomputers for access control and monitoring, this is appropriate and integral to physical security training).

A really good program for the protection of business information demands cooperative, tightly coupled work both by technologists and by physical security staff. Many times the systems staff will serve as a catalyst for a more effective consideration of information values, as systems design processes require rigorous definitions of protection needs.

3
PROGRAM CONCEPTS
AND STRUCTURE

A security program for computer-processed business information may be envisioned as a three-dimensional matrix. The three planes of the matrix consist of:

Top plane: exemplary computer user groups having protection requirements, usually differing among organizations, and perhaps consisting of

- business systems analysis and programming;
- research and engineering;
- office automation;
- data processing and telecommunications;
- time sharing, distributed processing, and distributed computing.

Front plane: the three levels of directive, as

- executive direction (policy);
- program management (standards);
- operating management (local procedure).

End plane: the four levels of protection, as

- physical protection;
- organizational protection;
- logical protection;
- transformational protection (usually encryption).

Figure 3.1 illustrates the program matrix.

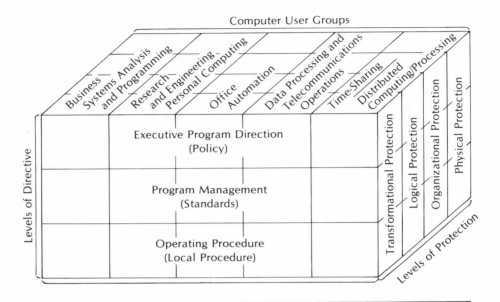

Figure 3.1.   Program structure, three-dimensional matrix. (Copyright, J. Schweitzer, 1980.)

THE THREE-DIMENSIONAL MATRIX

Levels of directive, in the front plane of the matrix, are established to allow flexibility in dealing with varying requirements and situations in a large business. In addition, the lower levels of directive permit management to cope with the nuances of technology. For purposes of a program for electronic information security, three levels of directive are used. These are illustrated in the program matrix in Figure 3.1. The top level is policy. Policy is a statement of limitations in a very broad sense. Policy stipulates some desired result with general guidelines as to achieving the result. A security policy might state that "all company information is private to the company, and will be provided sufficient security to guarantee that privacy."

Standards are the second level of directive. A standard establishes an operating mode, consistent with and supportive to policy. Standards apply across the company, in all divisions or units. A standard should represent a consensus, among those capable in the particular field of expertise addressed, as to the most desirable way of doing things. While standards establish common modes of action, they should also offer flexibility.

Good standards will provide flexibility to meet local operating situations, expressed through the lowest level of directive, called procedure. Typically, standards are used by system designers, and procedures are provided at the operating site for system users. There are many variations on this scenario, and that is the beauty of the three-level directive approach. A strong, resilient, practical security system can be built for all the situations and circumstances in which information processors are used.

POLICY, STANDARDS, AND PROCEDURE

Policy is the foundation of the program. Attempts at partial or local protection are not productive for the large business. The term "policy" as used here follows the definition given in *Webster's New Collegiate Dictionary:* "prudence or wisdom in the management of affairs; a definite course or method of action selected from among alternatives and in light of given conditions to guide and determine present and future decisions." Policy is then a general guidance from senior management as to courses of concern and action. Exactly "how" a thing is to be done is left to procedure, a lower level of directive. Policy is so important because it becomes the reference for lower levels of management at distant places and times, when immediate circumstances may require new or unusual courses of action.

Security policy must be based on a recognition that (a) the business has something to protect and (b) there are threats to the things to be protected. The first requirement to developing a policy proposal for management is the identification of the "things of value." That is accomplished through the information evaluation process described. Second, management must understand the general classes of vulnerabilities sustained by these valuable things (in our case, pieces of information or data). This may be provided through application of the general risk case as previously described.

Security policy may be viewed as being implemented at three levels:

Level 1:
- Policy at the top or corporate level. Brief, general statements for the guidance of lower level managers, or to restrict courses of action where appropriate.
  EXAMPLE: Employees are, in all cases, to be limited to accessing that information required for the discharge of assigned duties, as authorized by the employee's supervisor.

Level 2:
- Standards, at the middle or operating division level. Detailed statements of requirements established to insure coherent functioning of the corporation or the division.
  EXAMPLE: All access devices (terminals) will have hardware/software elements providing positive identification of the user.

Level 3:
- Procedures, at the lowest practical operating level, e.g., a data center or a telecommunications center, indicating specific, mandatory local practice in support of standard or policy.
  EXAMPLE: Terminal users in the research division must change personal passwords at least once each thirty days.

Each subsequent level of directive refers back to the one above. The "grandfather" directive, the policy, must be crystal clear in intent, and policy must have total management support at top levels. Any partial support or reservations will seriously weaken implementation of the policy throughout the organization, especially if senior line managers have doubts. It may be necessary to go to the top (the chairman, CEO, operating or managing director, etc.) to resolve all the security policy issues, but if so, it is a worthwhile trip. Figure 3.1 illustrates the policy levels graphically.

Characteristics of a Good Policy

A good policy will make clear the following minimum points:

- To whom does it apply?
- When is it effective?
- What is the subject and purpose?
- Who are the key participants (e.g., director of security)?
- How does it work?

A policy for electronic information security should address all aspects of a problem, and will be relevant to all appropriate audiences. The policy should

1. provide guidance to all those groups or functions using computers or telecommunications systems (and who may have unique requirements!);
2. be so constructed as to serve as a basis for the development of standards and procedures;
3. address current and near-future technologies, where the most serious exposures are likely; and
4. allow flexibility in the light of business requirements.

Many of the policies which the writer has seen have failed to include all these characteristics. Some examples of such failures include policies which cover the traditional data processing environment (data center, business systems development function) but do not include time-sharing or personal computing in the research environment. Policy may be written without broadly stated goals being evident, resulting in some people's (the ever-present exceptions to just about anything) being unable or unwilling to visualize the policy's applicability to their case.

Many policies on computer security deal adequately with today's situation, but overlook the fact that computing systems technology is developing at a fast pace. A policy written for a static world has little relevance to a business in dynamic change, as most businesses are.

Hard and fast requirements which may be seen by operating management as interference with primary business goals will be bypassed, in one way or another. Therefore, the policy must provide strength and flexibility to allow acknowledgment of critical business goals while retaining assurance of overall protection. Specific needs of user groups are addressed in detailed standards, which in turn are based on the policy.

Management Acceptance of Risk

Any business represents an entrepreneurial risk-taking. To impose a risk-free environment on a business may be an impractical, and certainly very costly, effort. Security policy should therefore allow managers at appropriate levels (depending on the risk involved) to decide to bear risk rather than expend resources on security. As in other weighty business decisions, managers responsible must have the fullest information on the potentials involved.

Essentially the question to be addressed is this: Are the costs of protecting against a given vulnerability so great that, given the worst-case exposure, it is preferable to bear the known risk? (Here is an opportunity to use a limited scope risk analysis.) Notice that this is analogous to many business decisions, where demand, product cost, market share, etc., are estimated to the best ability. Business is the taking of risks. Security policy must allow management to act responsibly with reasonable flexibility. Acknowledging and choosing to accept risk must be among the established alternatives. (Chapter 4 addresses one means of assisting management — Risk Analysis.)

A critical matter in this arrangement is the specification, in policy, of who can make the decision. Generally, a decision to take a risk concerning information at the highest value factor should be reserved for senior corporate executives or division presidents. Decisions concerning information with lesser value factors can be allowed at suitable lower organizational levels.

Developing Corporate Policy

The bedrock on which the program will operate is the corporate policy statement. The policy should be a general statement of goals and intent, based on a survey of the computer security literature and a knowledge of the particular methods and exposures of the business. At minimum, the corporate director of systems, the corporate auditor, and perhaps outside auditors should comprise a steering committee for drafting a policy proposal concerning electronic information processing security. The corporate security manager would serve as recorder and advisor to this group. (The reader is asked to substitute appropriate titles where necessary.) Once a proposed policy is agreed upon, it should be circulated among some division systems managers and controllers for comment. This process, or a similar one, will result in a policy statement which is acceptable to all.

The policy should, as far as possible, accommodate future technology applications, at least for the next five years. This is not difficult to do, as the policy is a general statement of intent. For example, a requirement for encryption of highly sensitive data in certain broad circumstances may be currently beyond the ability of the divisions. The policy statement, however, should drive the corporation toward the end posture desired. To do that, the policy must look forward. Remember that we will have an exceptions clause in the policy, as described earlier, so that unavailability of technology can be dealt with in a constructive way.

Exhibits 3.1 and 3.2 illustrate a policy and cover letter.

Exhibit 3.1.   Policy cover letter.

XYZ CORPORATION

Office of the Chairman

Subject: Security for Digital Information

To: Division Presidents

The Corporate Review Board has authorized a Digital Information Security program for XYZ Corporation.

Our increasing use of computers and telecommunications, in all divisions and at all levels of international operations, exposes critical business information to unauthorized observation, theft, modification, or destruction. I am sure you have read of such cases in the business press.

Your interest and support of this program will be necessary. Support in terms of funding and manpower will be required, some on an on-going basis.

I am attaching a copy of the new policy on digital information security. John Smith, Corporate Security Manager, will be providing you with detailed information on implementation and ongoing management of this important program.

XYZ CORPORATION
POLICY NO. 03-79
ELECTRONIC INFORMATION SECURITY

Purpose: To provide a consistent corporate-wide level of security for business information in digital form.

Scope: All operating divisions and headquarters, worldwide.

General: Information processed or transmitted via computing and electronic devices is
in digital form. Special security measures are required to protect this information. This
policy stipulates general means and goals for achieving such protection.

Policy requirements:

1. All business information, including personnel information, must be classified
   according to appropriate Risk Value Factors (see Policy 13-78, Business Information Value Classification).
2. All XYZ business information in Risk Value Factor Levels 1, 2, and 3 is to
   be restricted to those employees having a need to know by virtue of job
   assignments.
3. Access to digital business information in Levels 1, 2, and 3 will be controlled
   through access management systems as follows:
   a. initial access to a system will be through individual employee identifica-
      tion via password or similar;
   b. once connected to the system, employee must validate identity through
      an authentication method;
   c. identified and authenticated employees will be restricted to specific activ-
      ities by predetermined authorizations.
4. Level 1 business information must be encrypted when in storage or for
   transmission in digital form.

Exhibit 3.2.   Corporate policy

Security Standards: The Program Glue

Security standards are fairly detailed implementing instructions (see Exhibit
3.3) which insure a level of standardization and compliance with policy, across
the corporation. The standards should provide sufficient detail on requirements supporting the policy statements so that security coordinators and
operating managers can effectively make resource requirements estimations.

The division security coordinators play an important part in developing
standards. They may participate in any of several modes, including

- assignment of one of the various sections of the proposed standard to each security coordinator for development with subsequent review and concurrence by peers;

- forming a committee of security coordinators for review and approval of standards prepared at corporate level;

- any combination or similar method to obtain operating unit input.

All divisions should concur with the proposed standards before publication. This may require some tough "horse trading" by the manager of electronic security. Final agreement that the standards meet business requirements is important to later progress in complying with policy. (Table 3.1 shows the areas to be covered by standards.)

Table 3.1

**ELECTRONIC INFORMATION SECURITY STANDARDS
BY SUBJECT AREAS**

General
Information valuation
Information protection: marking and handling
Logical access management
Levels of protection
Security elements
Program management responsibilities

Data processing and telecommunications operation
Input and output processing
Facilities access controls
Management controls over operating environment
User services
Administration

Business systems development
Security requirements in phased development process
    Design
    Programming
    Installation
    Review

Office systems
Professional work stations
Word Processing
Distributed office systems
Facsimile and reprographics systems

Engineering and research systems
Personal terminals
Minicomputers
Laboratory computing

One is tempted to issue corporate standards immediately and thus avoid a lengthy, perhaps tedious process. Do not do it — the knowledge of the unit security coordinators about actual operating requirements and problems is a necessary input if good standards are to be developed.

Good standards mean reasonable, practical requirements which *will* be implemented at the unit or division level. Exhibit 3.3 shows a typical set of standards for electronic information security.

Exhibit 3.3. Standard

A. BASIS

To fix requirements supporting corporate policy, and to provide alternatives for activities in protecting information in electronic and other forms.

B. OVERVIEW

This standard addresses the protection and handling of value factor information processed or stored and applies to

- Business systems.
- Scientific and engineering activities.
- Data processing and telecommunications centers.
- Office use of computers and automated devices.
- Use of service bureaus.

C. TERMS USED IN THIS STANDARD

Value Factor 1 (VF1) — disclosure of this information could cause serious damage to the company. The existence and content of VF1 information is limited to those persons specifically designated.

Value Factor 2 (VF2) — disclosure of this information could have a detrimental effect on the company. VF2 information is disseminated on a "need-to-know" basis.

Prime System User — the manager authorizing system development or operation.

System User — the operator, solo programmer, or user of systems, computers, terminals or devices.

Digital Access Control Levels:

- Identify — claim to be a particular individual.
- Authenticate — proof of the above claim.
- Authorize — confirm approval to do certain things (read, modify, etc.).

Rationale — when VF information is stored, processed, or transmitted using computer devices, the information is in electronic (digital) form. Security requirements are similar to those for VF information on paper.

Exhibit 3.3   Standard (continued)

Protection requirements may be easily understood using this chart:

Medium Security Measures

	Identification	Storage	Distribution	Access Control	Destruction
Physical (Paper) Form	Originator decision, marking	Locked cabinet	Double envelope	Covered document limited use	Records retention schedule
Electronic (Digital) Form	Originator decision, prime system user decision, physical and logical labels	Locked cabinet	Special label, authorized courier, encryption (VF1)	Identification, authentication, authorization	Same as above

D. POLICY IMPLEMENTATION REQUIREMENTS

General - information is proprietary to the corporation, and certain security elements ensure integrity and security.

1. VF information is limited to employees authorized to have such information.

   When VF information is processed, stored, or transmitted in electronic form, security systems must be in place. If several users share resources, procedure to track authorizations, job assignments, and password changes will be provided.
   - It will ensure periodic changes of passwords and change accesses approvals when job assignments change.
   - Allow the Prime System User or System User to modify or change authorizations.
   - Provide records.

2. Systems Users have primary responsibilities for the security of the information processed. This responsibility requires timely information classification decisions. System Users must provide security features external or integral to the system, and/or selected from the features offered by the data processing and telecommunications centers.

   - Overall security in each case will include elements from each of the following levels:

     Level 1 Physical security (facility access control, employee identification, etc.)
     Level 2 Procedural security (separation of duties, control over changes to systems, etc.)
     Level 3 Hardware and software security (access control methodology, separation and insolation methods, etc.)
     Level 4 Encryption capabilities for VF1 information.

Exhibit 3.3   Standard (continued)

- The combination of protective elements to the system must protect to a degree suitable for the information.
- As a minimum:
  VF1 information: — four levels
  VF2 information: — levels 1, 2, and 3

- Required use of elements from each level are set forth in this standard. Local management may select a combination of elements, within the minimums, which will provide suitable protection. The measures must

  - be in effect at all times;
  - be capable of resisting attack;
  - protect multiple defenses;
  - include a monitoring facility.

- Managers shall implement formal action programs which ensure that these requirements are met.

BUSINESS SYSTEMS
1. *General* — systems design and development organizations are responsible for assisting the Prime System User in meeting requirements for the protection of VF information.

2. *Design* — Simplicity of programs enhances security. Controls must be provided which ensure integrity and completeness and which call attention to errors or attempts at unauthorized access.

- System design principles which support security:

  a) Security features must be described in documentation.
  b) Security features must be acceptable to the users, for practical everyday application.
  c) Every authorized user must be restricted to the actions necessary to accomplish the assigned task.
  d) When situations not anticipated occur, the system must continue to provide protection.
  e) Systems documentation must provide detailed instructions for the administration and control of passwords, and other functions.
  f) Terminal/network systems implementation package must include instructions for users on the identification and control of information which may be created via terminals.
  g) Accordingly, systems design specifications must indicate the management controls provided to the System User which will
     - provide review and approval of system changes;
     - ensure Prime System User control over the distribution of outputs.

Exhibit 3.3   Standard (continued)

3. *Programming*

- Practices — simple, modular program constructions, and limitation of programs to reasonable length are important to containment of risks. Testing shall be accomplished via "base case" data.
- Control — a control mechanism (passwording) will restrict programmer access to data files as authorized.
- Installation — before programs are used, the programming manager will advise the Prime System User of any security requirements that are not in place. The Prime System User will provide direction to (1) delay implementation, (2) obtain temporary exception approval, or (3) follow Exception procedure of this standard.
- Changes — management approval and authorizations will be obtained of all program changes. Authorization will include sign-off by the Prime System User and programming management *before* such changes are installed as a part of the permanent operating environment.

    Methods for handling emergency changes on some interim basis which ensure adequate approvals after the fact, but before (1) changes become permanent or (2) are applied a second time, will be installed.
- Documentation — access to documentation shall be controlled and limited to those employees requiring such information.

4. *Procedures*

Effective systems security includes all activities in a system, including input, processing, output, and distribution of output.

- Procedures must specify the checks and balances to maintain integrity.
- Each system must have procedures to control all changes to the system operating environment. These include changes to manual processing, operating documentation, or instructions.
- Procedures must ensure proper identification, marking, and handling of VF information.

    a) Each page of a VF report must be numbered and the last page so noted. Each page must be stamped or printed with a VF indicator in the upper right-hand corner as follows:
    VF1
    VF2
    each character is to be at least ½ " high.
    b) Microforms must have VF marking of a size to be noted by the human eye.
    c) CRT screens must include program-generated marking above with separation from other elements.

Exhibit 3.3   Standard (continued)

DATA PROCESSING AND TELECOMMUNICATIONS SERVICES

- General Security Requirements

  Data processing and telecommunications centers shall provide a variety of security features. These features shall be sufficient to allow Systems Users, directly or through their servicing systems organization, to select a combination of security elements suitable to the security requirements of the information being processed or handled.

  Upon request, data centers or telecommunications units will provide a description of available security features for the use of systems users and system designers.

- Environmental Security

  All data centers and communications centers shall

  - Establish positive access control systems which limit entry to authorized employees or authorized visitors. Entry/exit logs of all visitor traffic must be maintained.

    - Establish controlled areas or zones to which access is further restricted to specific employees (magnetic media storage areas, contingency storage areas, computer processing areas, etc.).

- Input/Output Functions

  - VF information must be protected from casual observation at all times.
  - Outputs must be marked and handled as required by this standard. VF output must be double-wrapped, with the inner wrapper stamped with the assigned classification.

- Data Centers and Telecommunications Operations

  - Data centers and telecommunications centers will actively supervise all activities, including control and prior approval of

    1) all operating system maintenance;
    2) all hardware maintenance;
    3) all initial processor loading or equivalent;
    4) all setting of system clocks;
    5) all changes to operating documentation, e.g., runbooks, job tickets, processing instruction, etc.

  - Activity logs, console logs, etc., shall be sequentially numbered and retained for 90 days or per records retention schedules or otherwise controlled to ensure a complete and auditable review of all actions.

Exhibit 3.3   Standard (continued)

- Magnetic Media Control

  All data centers and telecommunications centers shall

  - protect and control media by means of physical identification and the provision of a secure, controlled environment facility;
  - ensure that any shipment or transfer of such media is via courier, insured express, sealed mail, or equivalent;
  - protect media when being moved between locations. The classification of VF media must be marked on the container or reel;
  - maintain records of status, location, and disposition of each media item at all times;
  - degauss or shred each media device before transfer to others or disposition as waste;
  - inventory periodically to reconcile all media items to the records.

RESEARCH AND ENGINEERING USE OF COMPUTERS AND DEVICES

Users of minicomputers, computer and telecommunications terminals, distributed processors, and similar devices in the research, engineering, and development communities have special security responsibilities. Scientific/engineering/research managers at all levels responsible for, or having subordinates who operate, computers or similar devices shall

- provide instructions on the identification, marking, and handling of VF information which may be produced;
- establish individual employee responsibility for controls or administrative procedures which (1) limit access to information as required per job assignment, (2) specify those actions which authorized employees may take (e.g., read only, update, modify, execute program).

OFFICE ELECTRONIC SYSTEMS

Users of minicomputers, professional work stations, terminals, typing systems, displays, and similar devices in an office environment have special security responsibilities.

1. Managers at all levels responsible for, or having subordinates who operate, such devices in an office environment shall

   - provide specific detailed instructions on the identification, marking, and handling of information which may be produced where display devices show VF information, shielding of displays to prevent casual observation is required;
   - establish procedures to limit employee access to information in electronic systems to that required by virtue of job assignments.

USE OF VENDOR/CONTRACT SERVICES

Should vendor/contract services be required, the exception procedure in *Exceptions* applies and special security considerations arise. Decisions to use vendor/contract ser-

Exhibit 3.3   Standard (continued)

---

vices must consider costs and alternatives in light of security exposures. Use of vendors and/or contract employees requires

- inclusion of risks and vulnerabilities as a part of the decision to contract;
- supervision of such activities, to include regular review of security systems offered by vendor;
- that passwords issued to a vendor must be canceled immediately upon completion of a contract;
- legal agreements to protect information.

EXCEPTIONS

The Prime System User, upon determining through analysis that extraordinary difficulty or cost would be incurred in meeting this standard, may
a) request exception to this standard, supported by a formal risk analysis from the responsible division or unit executive; or
b) a corporate review of approval for exception to this standard will be provided by the Corporate Security Manager.

Regular meetings of the unit security coordinator with the manager of electonic security are important, especially in the early, formative stages of the program. In larger companies, some sort of regular newsletter or memo from the security manager is recommended. This newsletter can be very informal, but should contain technology developments, top management outlooks on security, and information on the planned meetings and subjects, and should also serve as a cross-fertilization medium. The unit or division security coordinators are both the developmental mechanism for the program and the means for insuring its strength and capabilities. The network of security coordinators may be viewed as the skeleton of the program; the standards and unit procedures are the muscle. Without the framework of the security coordinators, constantly developing and implementing technology application changes, the program will become a redundant, dead issue. Once electronic security standards have been agreed upon and published the security coordinators should be asked to do a detailed survey. This we will call a requirements survey. The operating divisions or units can now make fairly specific estimates of resources and costs, as they have the published security standards as a yardstick.

Some Special Cases;
or: These Will Get You If You Don't Watch Out!

The standards developed to implement the policy requirements must address the unusual cases as well as the typical uses of digital electronics in offices, data centers, applications programming, and scientific and engineering environments. Some of the special cases, where circumstances often create high risks, follow.

The Use of Contractors (Consultants, Temporary Help, etc.). Very often businesses in technological subjects will turn to contractors to do elements of work. Usually this is because the contractor has the expertise and employee skills needed by the business. When contractors have access to information with an established value factor, great care must be used to limit contractor employee access to that information required for the given task and cancel all access authorizations promptly upon completion of the work. The corporation may wish to establish contractor responsibility for data privacy through contractual means, e.g., nondisclosure agreements (there are standard legal forms available for this purpose).

The Use of Vendors. Data processing vendors, such as service bureaus or time-sharing service companies, may offer attractive service and cost benefits. Generally, this is because the user is participating in a joint depreciation of software investments, with other users. Whenever sensitive information is placed in a computer or on computer files outside the physical control of the owner, a severe security hazard exists. Actual cases have been reported where ex-employees of a vendor remotely access user files. The people had surreptitiously taken note of user passwords before resigning from the vendor's employ. A number of key requirements for those considering the use of vendors may be established:

1. Make certain the vendor's security posture is equal to that of the user. Most reputable vendors and service companies have superior security systems, but you must check to be sure (if not certain, include security in the contract and insist on the right to monitor the vendor's procedure).
2. Issue detailed instructions to using employees on how to use vendor security options. Usually, various levels of access control are provided, but actual application in a particular case is optional. Users will often ignore these security measures because they are seen as inconveniences. Standards must require their use to a degree consonant with policy.
3. Periodically visit the vendor's site and review his security measures.

SECURITY ELEMENTS AND LEVELS OF PROTECTION

Every security system contains multiple levels of protection. Even on the personal level, the individual's security system has several levels. Depending on the individual, these levels may be (1) avoid trouble, (2) run away, (3) fight back, and (4) accept attack while minimizing bodily harm.

Various levels of protection may be implicit in many security systems, but for the purposes of electronic information security, the levels should be expressed explicitly. These levels are shown in Figure 3.2 as a series of concentric circles. Conceptually, penetration through each succeeding level inward should be increasingly difficult. In practice, one or more levels may be bypassed by a penetrator, as we shall see.

Levels of Protection

The right-end plane of the three-dimensional matrix in Figure 3.1 shows the security elements required for the protection of digital information as occurring in four levels. The levels are related to the characteristics and placement of the security elements. Levels 1, 2, and 3 are always required for the protection of any information having an established value factor. Level 4, Transformation, is required only is special cases of a high value factor (see Chapter 1, Information Valuation).

Figure 3.2.   Concentric levels of protection.

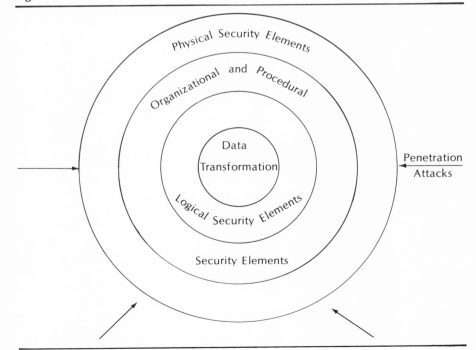

Level 1.   Physical security, or the separation of physical assets from potential harm, is a basic need for any kind of security program, and it is the underpinning for a computer-processed information security program. Level 1 refers to all those security elements which are necessary to insure that unauthorized persons are excluded from physical spaces and assets where their presence represents a potential threat. All types of computers, computing devices, and the associated communications facilities must be considered as sensitive assets and spaces, and protected accordingly.

Physical security elements include, but are not limited to, the following:

1.   Physical access controls, including guards/receptionists, door access controls (keys, magnetic cards, digital code keypads, voice recognition, hand recognition, employee badge examination), restricted areas (special authorization required), perimeter lighting and fencing, high-strength glass, closed-circuit television monitors, automatic door controls, and man traps.
2.   Locks and special protective features on cabinets, closets, compartments, etc., for protecting magnetic media (tapes, disks, cartridges) and reports containing information with established value factors. Vault-type doors for media libraries, laboratories, and other sensitive areas also fall into this category of physical elements.

Level 2.   Organizational and procedural security elements[6] consist of those arrangements of employee interfaces which will insure integrity and security of assets. Organizational and procedural elements include:

1.   Organizational compartmentalization to provide a series of checks and balances. For example, the electronic data processing auditors should not report to the senior data processing executive, but rather to the corporate treasurer or some other disinterested senior fiscal officer. This will help objective reporting of exposures. In a data center, data control (which validates outputs) should be separate organizationally from the computer operations producing those outputs.
2.   Procedural assignments which will provide a check on integrity and security. For example, computer tapes being selected for a process by the tape librarian are also checked, before operation, by a quality assurance function. After the production run, output tapes are checked by data control and by the librarian. (The obvious analogy is the cashier and the daily cash count by a second party.)

Level 3.   Logical security elements[7] consist of those hardware and software features provided in a system which helps to insure the integrity and security of data, programs, and operating systems (for which the references offer details). Such logical elements may include:

1. Hardware elements which segregate core and thus present overlap, accidental or intentional; core clearing after a job to prevent the following job seizing control; levels of privileges which restrict access to the operating system programs; hard-wired (firmware) programs which are not software-modifiable, and similar.
2. Software elements which provide access management capabilities. These are the key security elements in a program for the protection of electronic information. An effective logical security system provides the means for the identification, authentication, and authorization, or limitation, of the authenticated user to certain previously stipulated actions, for each system user who may "sign on" and/or for each program which may be called upon by the computer for purposes of processing files with established value factors.

Passwords are the most commonly used method for controlling access to computers and information serviced thereon. A password is similar to an unlisted telephone number. Some people know the number (e.g., the telephone company employees) because they must process it; other people are given the number by the principal (owner of the telephone). Both cases can negate the privacy value of the unlisted number by exposing it, or by using it in ways the principal will not like.

Most passwords are merely words or numbers selected by the user of the computer. In some cases the computer itself provides the password. In either instance, the password is usually private to an individual. If the user divulges the password to others, or exposes it so that other people know it, the password's efficacy as a security element is compromised or destroyed.

The most serious weakness of passwords relates to a common human failing, forgetfulness. People write the passwords on their desk blotters, in telephone list finders, on the walls, or even on the terminals so that they will not have to depend on memory.

The majority of passwords in use will be found to have characteristics of personal significance to the user. This means that the passwords are easy to deduce, especially for someone with training. Given names, children's names, birth or wedding dates, and home addresses are all very popular, because most users remember those things readily.

In today's systems, a single password is often the only security element between the would-be penetrator (an unauthorized user) and an entire array of data files and processes. This is similar to the lock on the typical house — once a penetrator is inside, all the contents are available. In computing, this is an extremely hazardous arrangement. Many of the vulnerabilities associated with passwords result from one or more of a set of common failings, as follows.

Passwords are improperly constructed, in that they are obvious or easily deduced, or have so few characters as to be subject to statistical attack (i.e., there are too few possibilities).

Passwords are never, or very seldom, changed. Even if a password owner takes "reasonable" care of the password, over a period of time it will become known to others. This may occur because of careless talk, observation of password key-in, failure to protect security listings of passwords, or accidential or intentional penetration to password files.

Passwords are not kept private. Often, password owners share access with others because of business requirements, camaraderie, or carelessness. While sharing may be only mildly vulnerable, unless the password is promptly changed it may be assumed that the password will quickly become general knowledge throughout the department or area.

Access management is the generic name for the set of security elements developed and applied for the purpose of controlling access to information. An effective access management system has three parts or functions, as follows:

1. A claim to be a certain person — an individual wishing to access information on a computer enters an *identification* code.
2. A proof of the claimed identity — the individual offers something inherent (voice print, for example), something known (password), or something possessed (a plastic magnetically encoded card) as *authentication* of the claimed identity.
3. The computer or communications system determines the allowable actions for that individual. A preset table or list is referred to, providing *authorization* for the individual to see, move, change, or operate on information in certain files or with certain characteristics. Any or all functions may be authorized by the "information owner."

Passwords are traditionally used for the identification and authentication steps in the access management process. A typical sequence would be:

SIGN ON
ACCOUNT NUMBER: 12345A (identification)
PASSWORD: J. ARNOLD (authentication)
SELECT FUNCTION: READ
SELECT FILE: ABACUS 3 (authorization)
ABACUS 3 NOT VALID. TRY ANOTHER (attempt rejected, not authorized)

In this typical case, the account number is really not a security construct as it is probably publicly known (within the organization of the password owner). The password itself is very weak, as it is probably a name related directly to the password owner. It will be deduced easily.

If the computer system does not automatically require password changes, the password "J. ARNOLD" has probably not been changed for years. A recent study by a large organization showed that 80 percent of its passwords had a "most recent change date" of 1978. That was when record-keeping was started! In such a case we must assume that both the account number and the password in the example are known, and are hence worthless as security elements. In fact, they are dangerous, because they give the impression of security but in fact offer none against someone familiar with the system and intentionally trying to penetrate.

Improving access management.   Passwords can be strengthened by improving the quality of the passwords themselves, and by combining passwords with supporting security elements. A password system of high quality has the following characteristics:

1. The password has at least seven characters in it. Mathematically, a password of seven or more characters offers great resistance to statistical attack. (We have to assume that an attempted penetration has computing support.)
2. The password is randomly constructed and has no relationship to the owner's environment. It contains nothing relatable to the owner's person, family, company job, etc. (and could be computer-generated).
3. The password is protected in a manner consonant with the value factor of the information being protected.
4. The password is changed regularly. In most cases, the password should be changed at least once every three months. (In one actual case, persons having obtained passwords illicitly were able to use them six months later, to steal computer services.)

People in the business environment are unlikely to be motivated to ensure effective passwording. People just do not want to be bothered. Some complementary measures which strengthen password effectiveness are:

1. Program the security software system to force password changes and automatically cut off people attempting trial-and-error access after x number of tries.
2. Provide administrative tracking of password changes, based on printouts from the computer system which show dates when last

password change occurred. The security coordinator can then follow up to remind computer users to change passwords.

3. Store all passwords in encrypted computer files. Passwords transmitted over communications circuits should always be in encrypted form.
4. Printing or display should always be suppressed when passwords are entered to a terminal keyboard.
5. A transform can be used as a "handshaking" procedure. In this method, the user has established a formula, such as $X = 3A + 10$. The computer would offer a value for A; the user, being the only person knowing the formula, would respond with a value for X.

Probably the most important factor in an effective passwording scheme is the will of the password owners to make it work. Chapter 1 discusses the importance of motivation. Data transformation, or encryption,[8,9] is used to provide ultimate protection for information with a high value factor, whenever such information is in storage on magnetic media or is in transmission via a telecommunications system. The Data Encryption Standard, from the U.S. Bureau of Standards, is the most widely accepted and the only certifiable means for encryption in the business world. Other algorithms are available and some are no doubt excellent. Encryption may be implemented by hardware or software, and costs will decrease as chip implementations become common.

Correctly implemented encryption of data is a means to several ends. Encryption may be used to[10]

1. prevent unauthorized observation or theft of information;
2. insure that delivery of a message or data stream is made only to the party intended (i.e., the one with the key);
3. authenticate an identity as the true sender or receiver of information (again, one who holds a key).

All these assurances are important in terms of maintaining information integrity and security. One could be assured, for example, that a formula transmitted was in fact that sent by the originator; that a funds transfer was accurate; that a message was genuine, etc. Encryption provides a security envelope similar to registered mail: not tampered with, not read, and guaranteed delivery to a specified person, with "signature" as proof of originator.

WHAT IS ENCRYPTION?

Encryption is the use of the ancient science of cryptography (literally, "secret writing") for information processing security requirements (in the sense used here, "information processing" includes computer application systems, tele-communications and data networking, computer terminals and communicating office equipment, and the use of all types of magnetic storage media). Cryptography has been a military art throughout most of recorded history. More recently, a science of cryptography has developed as a result of demands from the community of computer users.

Encryption is accomplished through the coding/decoding of information by using mathematical formulae (algorithms) and secret or public keys. A myriad of methods exists for performing encryption, based on various mathematical principles and properties. The system chosen should

- protect in the environment used (e.g., against the level of threat);
- provide protection at a cost acceptable to the user (typically, processing overhead);
- not interfere with business operations.

Table 3.2 provides a glossary of encryption terminology.

In practice, data encryption is achieved through the use of an appropriate algorithm and a key. The algorithm is a set of rules or steps for performing a specified operation (encoding). The algorithm may be processed by

---

Table 3.2
A GLOSSARY OF ENCRYPTION TERMS

Algorithm: A set of rules for performing a task.

Cipher: A form of cryptography employing a transformation of the information itself, based on a key, as the means of concealment.

Ciphertext: The results of enciphering plaintext.

Cryptography: The science of secret writing.

Decipher: To transform, using a key, from ciphertext back into plaintext.

Decrypt: To transform unintelligible information into intelligible information.

Encipher: To transform, using a key, from plaintext to ciphertext.

Encrypt: To render information unintelligible using a transformation algorithm.

Key: The secret controlling variable of an encryption algorithm specifying a particular transformation.

Plaintext: A readable message or data before encryption or after decryption.

---

a programmable piece of computer equipment or a set of electronic circuits can be constructed to perform the computations (hardware-implemented software).

The key is the "secret" part of the encryption system. Having a key enables a person or computer to encrypt or decrypt messages (data streams). Everyone may know what the algorithm (formula) is, but only those so authorized should have the key. Since there typically are hundreds of billions (2^{56}) of keys available for a reliable encryption algorithm, there is little fear that someone may guess or chance upon the key.

The key is typically a very large number (ten to twenty digits in length). The keys may be computer generated as random numbers. The confidentiality of the sensitive data may depend on the protection given to the key. For example, network control devices (minicomputers) may be used to create and distribute keys as required without any human knowledge of the keys. In the "public key" system, one part of the key may be publicly known, as are telephone numbers, associated with the "owner's" name. See below for a description of this system.

In recent years (since 1970?) government and business have recognized the hazards in the growing traffic of information on and among computers and computer devices. For the first time, nonmilitary applications for encryption technology have been recognized. The U.S. Department of Commerce, through the Institute for Computer Sciences and Technology at the National Bureau of Standards, initiated an effort to provide a standard for data protection during transmission or while in storage. In conjunction with IBM Corporation, the Data Encryption Standard was developed. This algorithm has been adopted as the standard for the United States. As a result, techniques and devices are now being commercially developed for purposes of implementing computer-based encryption systems.

The algorithm used in an encryption system need not be kept secret if well designed. An important part of an effective encryption security method is that everyone knows how it works and recognizes the difficulties in breaking its code. The cipher key, of course, must be kept secret. The key should be classified at the same level as the data it protects. Although truly unbreakable systems can be devised using one-time keys of a length greater than the text, this is impractical in the business situation. Today's encryption systems, in use in commercial applications, use fixed-length, relatively short keys, which are used many times except where key generation is automated.

The systems assume that a would-be penetrator has plaintext and ciphertext of the same message with which to determine the key. The strength of an effective cryptosystem lies in the probability of such success, which is so small as to require enormous computer resources to make an attempt with reasonable hope of penetration. The system, then, can always be broken given sufficient effort; the defense lies in the time, effort, and resources the penetrator must expend to break the code. This "work factor" applies to all security mechanisms. That is, no security system is impenetrable, but rather is considered sufficient if an attacker must use resources whose cost is unacceptable to him in light of anticipated gain.

The algorithm used to encipher information is considered acceptably strong, in terms of the work factor it provides, if

1. the mathematical equations describing the algorithm's operation are so complex that, for all practical purposes, it is not possible to solve for the key using analytical methods; and
2. it is too costly to employ methods which are mathematically less complicated because too much time is required, as in the case of key exhaustion, or too much data storage is required, as in the case of certain statistical attacks.[11]

As in the design of any defensive mechanism, assumptions are made concerning the capabilities and resources of the attacker:

1. Relatively large amounts of plaintext (specified by the analyst, if so desired) and corresponding ciphertext are available.
2. All details of the algorithm are available. (It is assumed that cryptographic strength must not depend on a requirement to maintain the secrecy of the cryptographic algorithm.)
3. A number of large high-speed computers (determined by the resources available to the opponent) can be used for cryptanalysis.

In the case of computer processed information, the work factor may be considered sufficiently rigorous if solution of the key identity is computationally infeasible, i.e., if it would require an inordinate resource or time, or the method for doing the problem is unknown to the mathematical community.

There are many different methods which may be used to implement an encryption method. In computer information processing, stream ciphers and block ciphers are used, primarily because these methods lend themselves well to binary notation and the operating characteristics of computer systems, and more importantly, because they provide great strength of security.

Using Encryption

Attacks against business information in computer-based systems fall into three categories.

1. Wiretapping, or the collection of information through physical connection or radiation evaluation. The penetrator records a bit stream and then may analyze the data, more or less, at leisure.

2. Terminal penetration, where the attacker uses inherent system weakness to discover passwords or to manipulate the operating system or the security system itself. The penetrator can see or destroy files, plant time-driven programs to do various clandestine tasks, or create self-destruction schemes affecting the hardware reliability, software accuracy, and data output integrity.
3. Physical theft of information on magnetic media, through actual removal from company premises, or by surreptitious copying and removal of the copied media.

In the categories described, the use of encryption increases the penetration work factor (cost to penetrate) enormously.

Achieving Protection.   Although wiretapping generally cannot be prevented, some types of attack can be reliably detected through good communications protocols. These attacks include message stream modification, denial of services, and spurious connection. Other wiretapping, which includes observation of message information and analysis of traffic patterns, cannot be detected, but damage may be limited through proper use of encryption. In all cases, attainment of security goals is based on the difficulty the penetrator faces in attempting to defeat the encryption algorithm.[12]

Terminal-originating penetration attempts result from weakness in the operating system, failure to administer the security subsystem, employee error and laxity, and incomplete or ineffective access management systems. There is no way to guarantee that penetration will not take place. The encryption of high value factor business files assures that the penetrator who can cut through the security subsystem to access on-line information files will get only gibberish for his trouble. (Data in work spaces of a computer are always cleartext and a penetrator into such work space is not affected by encryption.)

Surreptitious removal of correspondence or data files stored on magnetic media is essentially a matter of good physical security and office discipline. Proper media control requires item numbering, inventory records, careful placement, and active management. In spite of these security elements, people do and will remove magnetic media from business premises for varying purposes, some of which may be illegitimate. (This vulnerability will become increasingly severe as the "advanced electronic office" develops; it is already serious in data centers). If the information on the media (tapes, disks, etc.) is encrypted, the unauthorized possessor will not be able to decipher the data contents.

A clear, readily demonstrated rule on the alternatives of implementation of encryption, in terms of hardware versus software, is impossible at this time. This is so because so many cryptosystems are being developed, and because all of the developments are in the early stages (first-generation products).

Generally, requirements should dictate the implementation method used. If relatively small amounts of data are to be encrypted for use by a small group of people, such as a time-sharing system with some sensitive files, a software implementation is probably the best. Original cost (for a commercial package) will be reasonable, and use will seldom be enough to avoid running up big overhead processing charges.

If large streams of data are to be processed, especially where a link or heavily used data path is involved, hardware is superior to software. Encryption hardware manufacturers are developing increasingly efficient, miniaturized products. Operating costs consist of a small overhead and the administration of keys (no small matter in a big network).

Hardware, at this stage, must be considered to be more secure than software, since there is reduced potential for already-present or induced software "bugs," i.e., the hardware cannot be modified easily. Also, software computation in support of either method is much more expensive than hardware implementation, and in some cases overhead can approach 100 percent.

Software-implemented encryption packages (encryption through the processing of a program of instructions) are commercially available. Some require typical key administration. Others (e.g., Raviv transform) use the statistical characteristics of the data to be encrypted, with a random number generator, to create internal keys. Since these keys are recreated whenever the particular data set is encrypted or decrypted, there is little or no key management effort involved. The keys are processed under protection of the encryption system, in encrypted form. Certain of these software packages generate keys with lengths equal to the data itself. As mentioned above, this is the most secure situation from the point of potential breaking of the cryptosystem.

The software encryption system is maintained on the computer program library along with other application programs. The encryption program is "called" and operates against the file to be encrypted or decrypted. The exact mode of activity is determined by the data set condition when the software encounters it, i.e., if data is encrypted, it is decryption mode and vice versa.

As is true with most security systems, encryption requires an administrative effort. If encryption is to provide real protection, a significant administrative effort is necessary to manage the control and distribution of the encryption keys. In a network security system, key administration can be automated, thus eliminating most manual effort but creating a systems cost.

Usually, two levels of keys are used; the terminology applied to the levels depends on the system or author describing the method. For a basic understanding, the keys may be regarded as the primary and secondary keys.

- Primary Key: The primary key (PK) is distributed by messenger or registered mail for entry to the encryption device or program. Its purpose is to authenticate secondary keys, thus avoiding the requirement to use a messenger or registered mail when a secondary key is to be changed. Each node or receive/send location may have a unique PK.

- Secondary Key: The secondary key (SK) may be changed as desired. The SK may be used for only one session or for discrete data flow. The SK may be changed every day, week, month, or otherwise periodically. In some cases, the SK may be used for only one message, then discarded. This is a high security method typical to the military/intelligence communities. When the SK is changed, it is encrypted with the primary key and transmitted as data to the receiving device or software. Since various nodes may have unique primary keys, even an interception or misrouting of a new SK would not compromise security.

The network security manager (or the automated network system controller) must maintain a safe file for storage of keys and must keep records of the keys used for various links, sessions, or locations. If an encryption key is confused or lost, the data are not recoverable. Therefore, efficient means must be established for key recordkeeping and protection.

Some manufacturers provide hand-held devices for loading the primary key. The device may be stored at each location in a safe. It then may be used to reload the primary key should a power or equipment failure require it. It is impossible to read out the primary key from the device, as it will generate only into a specified encryption module, and uses light emissions as a carrier. Tampering with the sealed device immediately destroys the key.

The key management process is somewhat different for each system, but a general procedure may be described as follows (an automated process follows a similar sequence):

1. After installation of the proper hardware or software, the responsible security manager (SM) generates one or more primary keys. The system will usually provide random number generator means for developing secure keys. Once the key is developed, it is read out, either into a portable loading device, as described above, or as a long series of digits which are hand-copied and protected.

2. The SM makes a copy of the primary key and places it in his safe with the necessary descriptive indications (where to be used, etc.). Complete records are necessary. The SM then delivers the primary key(s) to the locations required. These locations could be the ends of a communications link, nodes in a network, specific user offices, etc. Distribution of the keys, as high value factor information, is done by messenger or by registered mail.

3. At the receiving locations, the primary key is loaded into the equipment or software, by keying-in, or by use of the hardware device

described above. Documents describing the primary keys are then destroyed, locked in a safe, or returned to the SM, depending on the system chosen. For best security, only the SM should have a copy of the primary keys. (This is not true when a hardware loading device is in use. The device is always kept in a safe, however.)

4. Once primary keys are loaded, the SM may generate secondary keys, which are then sent to the proper locations as encrypted messages (encrypted with the primary key). If an acknowledgment is received from the receiving locations, the primary keys are successfully loaded and the system is ready to operate.

5. Routine encryption may commence using the secondary key to encrypt the protected data. Secondary keys may be changed as desired, using the primary key facility. More frequent changes of secondary keys increase cost and improve the security protection.

A manual procedure is described to illustrate the process. In practice, key generation, distribution, and management will probably be done by automated means.

Each level of protection in the three-dimensional matrix (Figure 3.1) contains a set of security elements, or features. These security elements are cumulative in the sense that they increase the penetration work factor (PWF), or the effort required of a penetrator, as discussed earlier. The PWF, or total effort required along with risk of discovery, will contribute to decisions by the penetrator as to method, time to be expended, value of results, liability if caught, and so forth. The PWF is a deterrent. A strong PWF, evident to the penetrator, means that the stakes must be high for continued penetration effort.

The PWF itself may indicate that, at best, only partial information will be obtained. A discouraged penetrator is a thwarted penetrator. Before discussing some cases where the PWF was ineffective, we can postulate some rules about security elements.

1. Electronic information security measures should be publicized. Their resistance to attack must not depend on the measures themselves being secret. For example, a password access control depends on a password construction of sufficient strength, plus frequent changes of passwords. The passwords themselves, of course, are secret. The procedure for providing and changing passwords should be publicized as a part of systems installation processes.

2. Sufficient security elements must be provided in each concentric level to insure that all avenues of penetration are covered. At the logical level, for example, access management control must be established over operating system software maintenance activities. There is little

to be gained in closing doors through identification and authentication measures controlling terminal access, if internal systems doors are unguarded.

Figure 3.3 illustrates the security elements. Keep in mind that an exhaustive list is impossible. Novel situations almost always result in new measures, which may represent elements not previously recognized.

The requirements for, applicability, and importance of the levels of protection and their security elements are best seen through the use of case examples. For each case, which has been developed from real-life situations, an analysis is provided. Keep in mind that there is no finite list of security elements. Those indicated in the analysis as being causal may have been incomplete in themselves, or improperly applied.

Case 1

Janice Smith was a sterling employee, intelligent, well motivated, and a whiz at programming. The data processing manager was disappointed when Janice resigned. A gala farewell party was held. Janice, however, did not feel as sorrowful at the parting as some others. She rented a terminal and set up a consulting business from her apartment, using her ex-employer's computer. Business was good. Janice became greedy and decided to store her customer's files on the computer, in addition to the programming which she had been doing. After a few months, the excessive use of disk file space became evident to the computer's owners. Janice's files were erased and her password was eliminated from the authorization file.

Analysis: Case 1

Levels of Protection	Status at time of Incident	Causal Situation
Physical	In place	Not relevant
Organizational-procedural	Weak	Failure to change authorization
Logical	In place	Ineffective due to procedural failure
Data transformation	Not used	

Level 1 (Outer)	Physical Security
Perimeter control:	fencing, lighting, access controls
Building control:	access control, visitor restrictions, badges
Area control:	inside restricted areas, access restrictions

Level 2	Organizational and Procedural Security
Organizational Security:	definition and separation of duties, shared responsibility
Procedural Security:	fiscal controls
	written procedure
	supervision
	work review
	process control
	materials control
	document marking

Level 3	Logical Security
Hardware Security:	functional separation of processes, read-only memory, core clearing
Software Security:	privileged instructions, access control subsystems access management packages, security kernel

Level 4 (Innermost)	Data Transformation
Encryption systems	
hardware:	communications link
	communications network
	write-to-media (channel control)
software:	write-to-media
	pretransmission
	callable programs

PENETRATION

Figure 3.3. Security levels and elements.

Case 2

ABC company used an on-line process control system. Modifications were continually being made because of product mix changes and varying characteristics of raw materials. Programmers made changes to the system programs by means of password-authenticated entry to the program library. Chris Allen was discharged by the programming manager at ABC because of poor attitude and job performance deficiencies. The following day, ABC programmers discovered they could no longer access the program libraries, the password file having been changed by persons unknown. An investigation showed that Chris Allen had been allowed to return to the programming work area for a period of time before leaving the ABC facility. System records showed the passwords had been changed from his terminal.

Analysis: Case 2

Levels of Protection	Status at Time of Incident	Causal Situation
Physical	In place	Not relevant
Organizational- procedural	Poor discharge procedure	Should have been escorted from facility
Logical	Poor security for password file	Should not have been able to change other than own password
Data transformation	Not used	

Case 3

Employees of a racetrack were able to modify programs on a backup computer and thereby generate winning tickets after a race was completed, but before the wagering results were computed. They in effect stole from the winners by adding more winning tickets to the number, splitting the winner's pool.

Analysis: Case 3

Levels of Protection	Status at Time of Incident	Causal Situation
Physical	In place	Not relevant

Levels of Protection	Status at Time of Incident	Causal Situation
Organizational-procedural	Poor supervision, poor procedure	Employees able to violate system procedure repeatedly
Logical	Weak security for operating system	Operators able to change data files and access privileged programs
Data transformation	Not used	

Case 4

A stockbroker planned to make a profit by obtaining information on strategic buying from a large competitor's files. He was able to identify a telephone line used for transaction data traffic. By climbing a pole, he tapped the line and copied off all the data traffic. Using a small computer, he was able to analyze the traffic and obtain information on volume buy orders before they were completed.

Analysis: Case 4

Levels of Protection	Status at time of Incident	Causal Situation
Physical	In place	Bypassed
Organizational-procedural	In place	Not relevant
Logical	Not applicable	
Data transformation	Not used	Encryption would have denied information to penetrator

These cases illustrate the common failings in security programs:

1. Security elements provided do not cover all the exposures. Some security elements are in place in every case; nevertheless, penetrators succeeded.

2. Security elements are not properly maintained or administered. Even
    though passwords or other access control methods are used, failure
    to change them at appropriate times negates their value as protective
    measures.

No security program, including the one proposed in this book, can provide
perfect security. But many businesses may have security coverage which is in
fact a placebo. The business managers feel secure, but are not. This is a very
dangerous situation, worse than the case where the business has no security
and is nervously accepting acknowledged risk.

Conclusion

A program for information security must include security elements in all four
levels of protection. The security elements must reasonably cover all the vulnerabilities, must be rigorous and offer resistance against attack, must pose a
significant work factor to the penetrator, and must always be in effect.

Specific details on a suggested standard were provided in Exhibit 3-3. A
selection of valuab,e options in security elements for the four levels of protection can be found in the References at the end of the book.

COMPUTER USER GROUPINGS

The computer user groups in the top plane of the matrix represent a convenience grouping which may vary according to the style and organization of a
business. For example, in some businesses, information processing activities
supporting business management functions (accounting, customer services,
etc.) are highly structured, while scientific information processing is largely
free-form. Security rules and practices for one group may be confusing to
another, because terminology is different. Office workers, for another example, have environments different from those of production or engineering
workers, although both may use terminals and automated office-type equipment. (Eventually, security will depend on individual motivation!)

The user groups, then, are a recognition of the need to provide security
requirements tailored to the work situation. The reader should anticipate a
need to define user groups according to the practices and organization of the
particular business.

People using computing in the various parts of a business view the computer differently. The view of one person may be completely different from
that of another. Hence, the computer security rules may be more effective if
provided in a context harmonious with the viewpoint of the computer user
audiences.

Consider a secretary, a scientist, and a programmer working on business systems. All three may use computers extensively. The secretary has an advanced office processor which does word processing, communications, and can retrieve data from a central file. The scientist has a terminal, almost exclusively used for mathematical processes, with a small printer. The business programmer is working at a terminal in a highly structured environment, developing programs which are part of a large system.

Each of these people is using a computer, but the working environment, vocabulary, and understanding of the basic technology applied differ widely. Preparing a security procedure to fit each group is more effective and "friendlier" than attempting to use a generalization. In the reader's business situation, the groups or their characteristics may vary from those discussed here, but the concept remains.

BUSINESS SYSTEMS

Business systems consist, for our purposes, of those applications (computer hardware, communications systems, and software) supporting the general processes of business. These processes include accounts payable and accounts receivable systems, manufacturing and inventory control systems, payroll and treasury systems, and customer and employee recordkeeping systems. Such systems are typically "batch processing." (For example, a payroll system where time tickets are processed or key-entered in batches, updating files and generating a "batch" of outputs, in one cyclical run.)

Separation of business systems from other types of computer applications is done to make description of security processes simpler. Many of the various types of systems may interface and exchange data; some may be closely coupled.

Segregation of business, research, office, and communications systems is done because experience has shown that the "audience groups" using these systems require different security approaches. Where business systems offer remote access to files via terminals, security is covered below.

From an electronic information security viewpoint, business systems may be considered to have five parts, related to the traditional systems life cycle. These parts are

1. business systems analysis and programming;
2. input processing;
3. data processing operations;
4. output processing;
5. maintenance.

Security in the Business Systems Development Process. Systems analysis and programming are key activities in the information security process. Security elements (as previously described) must be "built-in" to the business systems during the design process. From a management outlook, good control of business system development is closely related to good security. In other words, the use of a rigorous phased systems development process is critical both to investment control and to security.

In certain phases of development, where management review is provided, auditors or other reviewers representing management must ascertain that suitable security elements are included in the design and programming of the system. Table 3.3 illustrates phases and related security efforts.

The first of these security reviews must be at an early phase of system development. At minimum, a phase I or phase II review should establish that an information value factor for the data to be processed has been determined and that suitable (according to policy and standards) security measures are planned and described in the system specifications. The ability of the systems analysts and programmers to provide security mechanisms depends on the existence of adequate standards based on policy, as discussed earlier. The information security standards are then the basis for phase reviews of the security elements being built into the system.

Later phase reviews, at those phases addressing final testing and data center acceptance, must address the testing of the efficacy of the security elements in the real-life use of the system, both in terms of information processing and in the input/output activities closely related to process design.

Business systems documentation must include thorough instructions for the users and processors of system data concerning the electronic security measures required. The documentation should spell out, among other things, how access authorizations are granted and effected (e.g., how does a prospective user obtain approval to access data, and how does one get a password?);

Table 3.3
PHASED DEVELOPMENT AND SECURITY

Phase	Activity	Related info. security work
I	Requirements definition	Determine business sensitivity
II	System specification	Establish data value factors
III	System Engineering	Develop manual-logical access control procedure
IV	Test and installation	Security review and audit preinstallation Postinstallation security test
V	Maintenance	Audit System efficiency testing

who controls such authorizations; marking and control requirements for outputs, both hard and soft (CRT) copy (generally directly related to established value factor); and last, tape or other media retention and protection requirements.

The Business systems development process itself requires a significant level of security. Systems design documents, programming worksheets, program listing, and overall systems documentation should be provided security commensurate with the value factor assigned to the data to be processed. In other words, the systems documentation and program listings should be assigned value factor equal to that assigned to the system's information. This means that access to systems design and programming areas, on-line terminals, on-line files, documentation libraries, working papers, etc., must be restricted to those employees having a need to know by virtue of job assignments.

Business applications programming is a severe security risk in business today. In most companies, programmers operate in a "club" atmosphere, surrounded by mystery. One need only read any of the available books on programmer productivity to realize that programmers, by and large, are not managed today. Many will have carte blanche access to any systems or information, often via on-line terminals ostensibly provided for program maintenance and development. These terminals may also be used for secret programming to accomplish unauthorized ends. Good business practice and minimal security and data integrity require that all business programming be done in a controlled environment. Such an environment includes

- all testing and maintenance done via a "base case" or duplicate of the actual business files;
- all program maintenance changes approved by three levels of management:

  1. management of using function
  2. programming management
  3. data center management;

- all programmer access to a computer is through password-verified authentication mechanisms. (It is interesting to note that, contrary to initial reaction, controlled programming environments are well liked by managers once properly implemented. Good control is good management.)

Without these minimal control measures, management is literally turning business control over to the journeyman programmers.

An illustration of an information security standard for business data processing is shown in Exhibit 3.3.

PERSONAL COMPUTING

In this section we will deal with a phenomenon which will pose a novel threat. That is, the appearance of personalized computing through terminals, intelligent office devices, minicomputers, and attached communications processors. A subset of this user group occurs in the section below on Office Automation. The rapid development of miniaturized computing facilities, with tremendous capabilities, is delivering electronic information access, withdrawal, and computing powers to individuals at work, at home, and while traveling. Vast networks for purposes of disseminating information are being constructed or are already in service. This threat is particularly serious because of two factors involving the users and the electronic information available:

1. The people who are using or will typically use personal computing facilities have the knowledge and capabilities to mount successful, clandestine attacks on critical electronic information data bases. These are the high-grade knowledge workers, whose job requirements include detailed knowledge of one or more of the technical areas involved in the hardware and software construction of the information systems environment. In the general case, they must be assumed to be lacking only motivation for unauthorized activities — the capabilities are there.
2. The electronic information contained on network-connected systems may be of a sensitive nature. It includes financial analysis data, some in highly summarized form; research and development information; and, in advanced office systems, executive reports and correspondence.

The personalization of computing, implemented as local terminals or processors interconnected or as distributed computing (see discussion below), means that a large and varied population of users will have powerful equipment (in many cases ostensibly for entertainment or home uses), with potential for accessing important business information. An effective program for electronic information security may provide increasing protection as computing uses expand, but complete protection is probably impossible.

Business use of personal computing in its many forms means that not only do the authorized secretaries, managers, scientists, and engineers have access, but potential exists through common network connection for access by a wide range of hobbyists, home users, university people, and others. Increasing technical awareness leads to curiosity-driven or malicious attempts to access business files. Cases are on record of organized attempts by persons outside business to penetrate business computing networks for illegal purposes.

In this environment, the awareness and security consciousness of employees are most important, so that individually applied security measures will be effective. Logical security elements can limit penetrations by placing substantial barriers in the way of unauthorized people connected via networks. And properly applied encryption systems can provide robust security for the high-value information critical to a business (see earlier discussion).

RESEARCH AND ENGINEERING

Consider the researcher who is using a personal minicomputer to perform studies bearing on a new product. A breakthrough occurs — does the employee instinctively act to protect this information? Does he or she know how to mark, cover, store, and disseminate information with a high value factor? Remember, this may be novel information. No precedent exists for its value. The researcher may run down the hallways shouting to the world, "Eureka, I've found it!" and tell everyone who will listen. Or he may create a file and send it (electronically?) to everyone he hopes to impress. No consideration for security here. If the researcher is security-conscious and properly motivated, however, the information will be stored in a password-protected file. The password will be a new one, of sufficient strength to resist attack. Any reports produced will be marked and wrapped for delivery according to established information protection procedures. If the information is transmitted in electronic form to others in the research community (very likely in an automated R & D environment), it will be encrypted to ensure security or privacy. Similar scenarios can be imagined for offices, plants, and other business environments. The existence of the mechanics of a program for security, in themselves, just cannot do the job in the computer age. Employee motivation is the key to achieving information security, and the unit or division security coordinator is the prime mover in this effort.

Effective security for information processed and/or stored in the research and engineering environment requires carefully developed, well-enunciated standards. Such standards must recognize and emphasize the personal responsibilities of each computer user for the recognition and protection of information. Where appropriate, each user should have precise instructions on recognizing information values, which should result in the employee's providing protection to the information, whether in digital or human-readable form, commensurate with its value.

General rules concerning data centers and traditional applications processing do not apply here. One person may serve as system designer, programmer, operator, tape/disk librarian, output clerk, and ultimate user, and in fact may have a high-powered computing facility totally within the confines of his or her office or laboratory. Many researchers in technology-oriented industries may develop personal computing systems (hardware, software, or both) which may be portable, and thus allow the employee to work at home. In other cases, networks of powerful processors may be in use as mail systems, general computers, and graphics generators. When many of the operators of such a system understand its most esoteric workings, the security of the information processed depends wholly on employee motivation and training.

Special and unusual information security standards are required for these environments. The standards must provide clearly defined statements of responsibility and must offer the research and engineering user a menu of security measures, and these measures must be acceptable in the working environment. These unique security needs follow from the job tasks in these activities. Some examples:

- the scientific programmer, who is using computers or computerlike devices to measure physical or chemical properties (analog signals may be collected and converted to digital signals for analysis or storage);
- the system development engineer, who may have custom-built operating computer models, testing devices, minicomputers, or terminal devices connected to interlaboratory or interplant systems;
- the scientist or engineer who may have office computing via a desk minicomputer or by means of sophisticated, intelligent terminal (can process locally) access to a central system.

In all these cases, remarkable differences exist from the traditional business systems case. The scientific or engineering user does not have systems development controls. If security measures are to be imbedded in the local processing system, the user or originator of the custom system or programs must build in the security elements.

There is unlikely to be formal media library services, so that if the data on disks and tapes are to be protected, the originator must provide that protection, logically or physically. Underlying these basic requirements is a supposition that the scientific or engineering user of personal work station computing is security conscious and motivated to protect company information. Such protection must rely on personal willingness to make value factor decisions, e.g., does it need protection, and to what degree? Suitable standards should provide guidance to this audience.

The security coordinator for the research and engineering divisions or departments plays a key role in developing these standards. An understanding and keen appreciation of the research and engineering environment, with the cooperation and contribution of personal computing systems users, are absolutely necessary. Unfortunately, most security and data processing departments in business today understand very little about this environment and its needs.

OFFICE AUTOMATION

Security managers should consider office automation as a part of the overall development and application of computing technology rather than as a separate phenomenon. This view helps to see how security measures previously applied to data centers and the use of computer terminals can be modified and adapted to office automation. It is also probably the most accurate viewpoint in terms of computing science.

Computers have been used for years to automate clerical, repetitive aspects of traditional office systems, such as accounts receivable, accounts payable, payrolls, general ledger, and personnel records. Office automation means that miniaturization and computing economics have now provided computers which can be embedded in office systems hardware designed for personal, individual use. These new systems are designed to serve as personal, electronic substitutes for the administrative actions which have always required writing or printing on paper.

Office automation will provide systems which electronically create messages, text, and graphics; which store and retrieve files; which communicate with other systems across the room or across the world; and which can produce paper copies anywhere. Security considerations in the use of such systems fall into two general categories. The first is the effect of the application of automated office systems on people, which may result in loss of traditional roles, poor morale, or antagonism. The second area for security concerns is in the technology itself, which presents a new set of security vulnerabilities for business information which is stored and moved about in electronic form.

Effects on People

These high technology devices have implications equal in weight to those changes wrought by the computer in the 1960s. Managers must force rethinking of traditional business methods; systems analysts must open their minds to considering truly total systems, including the processing of written inputs or outputs at the ultimate user location, not just through the data center printer.

The most serious effect of the new devices is not that of changes to procedure; rather, it is the modification of the job criteria for the human resource. Any good systems analyst knows that a system cannot be successfully installed unless the people who are to operate the system want it to work. Perhaps the worst approach is to promise too much when technology is installed. One can postulate a number of concerns which must be of interest to managers and systems analysts and, of course, security managers.

First, the application of the new office technologies destroys the traditional (and sometimes professional) job positions in the office environment. Past high-value office employees have been skilled generalists, understanding and responding to implied directives, keeping things going, and minding to countless details. Consider such work as filing, preparing correspondence, making travel reservations, sending out mail. How often has anyone seen procedures covering these things? The skilled office employee has learned to read subtle signs, to remember certain goals, and to use judgment to respond. The executive who says, "My secretary is wonderful," is really saying that the secretary has the best interests of the business at heart, and responds to situations accordingly.

Technology does not allow for generalized responses and severely limits the application of judgmental decisions. So the office worker may have to change from a skilled generalist to a skilled technologist. Usually, this change will mean a narrower scope of work, but with more vertical depth. For example, where the clerical employee previously performed almost all the jobs in the office, that employee may now handle only communications, but may be involved from the initial dictation through the ultimate facsimile transmission and communication with the end recipient. This implies severe personal trauma for many who face these changes.

Second, the new office technologies change the economic relationship of the employee to the job. Investment in technology implies either greater throughput or lower operating costs, for otherwise the investment will not be made. In some cases, the application of technology will reduce the employee job content value and result in realignment of salary levels. One example of this is the automated duplicator. Previously, most companies used highly skilled printers to operate duplicating equipment, as setup and operation required fine tuning to achieve the proper mix of water, ink, paper, and pressure. The new duplicating equipment automatically senses when things go wrong and tells the operator in words just what to do about it. A low-grade clerical employee may easily be trained to operate one of these new machines.

Third, the use of high technology office systems may effect other functions as office procedure becomes more rigorously defined. Consider the matter of filing of correspondence. When the office converts to a magnetic or microforms filing system, a secondary system must be provided for those functions and outside business not communicating in modes which are compatible.

Fourth, the development and availability of combination equipment having the characteristics of minicomputer, network-connected terminal, and typewriter means that many of the present skilled, intuitive, or decision-making activities in the office can be automated. This will reduce the time required to do many of the routine tasks, and thus require fewer people. Those who remain will have to be able to operate and understand the systems involved. For example, travel reservations could be made directly with the airlines, with seat availability and confirmations appearing on the office terminal CRT.

All four concerns about office automation have security implications. These are not direct threats, such as that of software penetration, discussed below. Rather, they are implied threats developing from potential employee dissatisfaction or insecurity (see the earlier discussion on morale). The people who will be using automated office systems will probably have personal characteristics which should make them particularly interesting to the security manager. Typically, they will

1. be well educated and relatively young;
2. be above average in salary and potential;
3. have knowledge and capability to probe below the surface level of a system;
4. have no traditional constraints or controls in using the system, and those which do exist will be viewed by some as challenges;
5. be willing to take risks if an advantage is seen, with their greatest fear being that of embarrassment.

This profile is the same as that of the typical "computer criminal."[13,14] Generally, business management does not recognize this threat or prefers to ignore it when it materializes.

Much of the information used in the office via personal computing is or will be specially designed for use at decision-making levels of the business. For example, financial analysts may have access to central files of information which represent divisional or corporate "roll-ups" of year-to-date or monthly results. Executive secretaries may have access to key memos concerning very private business matters, even when those memos are not directly addressed to them or their boss.

Concerns from Technology

The human vulnerabilities resulting from office automation are of concern to the security manager, but a more serious and immediate exposure results from technology. Fortunately, this area lends itself more readily to available security solutions than does the human factor. Technology centers around the electronic form of information, which no longer has the time and spatial constraints associated with information in paper forms. Vulnerabilities resulting from technology in the automated office environment may be considered as those resulting from communications, storage and retrieval, change of mode, operating systems, and expansion of the trusted group.

Communications. The capability to communicate information swiftly to any connected unit on a network or interconnected networks (almost all networks are by virtue of public utility services!) is the essence of office automation. Time and spatial constraints associated with pieces of paper disappear as information may be sent to distant places with no recognizable time lapse. Such service implies use of long lines or radio links, both of which represent a most serious vulnerability for business information. The solution for this exposure is encryption of transmitted information between the originating point and the addressee.

Within the business facility, physical security must be provided for the communications connections boxes, gateway computers, modems, or other equipment which might allow an unauthorized connection.

Storage and Retrieval. Electronic office systems will allow information in text or statistics form to be stored locally or at a central site for later retrieval or sending to others. Local storage may consist of writing on a magnetic disk, tape, or cartridge. Central storage may use either disk, tape, or cartridge, but usually will employ on-line disks. Printing facilities may also have storage capabilities, if only for buffering purposes. All such magnetic storage causes security exposures. These risks occur because

1. the magnetic media themselves may be stolen or temporarily removed for copying;
2. many systems offer the capability for transfer of information among various media stations from a remote site, through issuance of certain commands;
3. local storage may be susceptible to clandestine "dumping" of contents by unauthorized persons who may have technical capabilities for bypassing usual controls.

Protection for storage systems lies in effective application of logical security methods (discussed earlier in this chapter) which limit access to authorized system users, and good physical security for tapes, disks, and cartridges which contain sensitive information.

Change of Mode. Whenever information changes from human-readable form to electronic (digital or analog) forms, a security risk develops. This is so because at that moment the information exists in one place in both forms. Control is more complicated and the opportunity for unauthorized change is ripe. Most cases of fraud result from unauthorized manipulation of a system at a point where information changes form, such as at a bank teller station or where an accounts receivable clerk is entering payments.

Another obvious exposure is in the office, when a secretary types a paper copy and at the same time enters an electronic record, perhaps for communication to a distant place. The information is then in four forms: the original, hand-written paper (if used), the ribbon for printing, the disk or cartridge used as storage of buffer, and the paper output. A good system is required to protect all these forms effectively, which will apply physical, logical, and encryption methods.

Operating Systems.   All complex office systems have operating systems, or executive systems, as either hardware electronics or program software loaded into disks. Computer science has not yet been able to provide error-free "certified" operating systems, so that all software requires maintenance. This need is a security exposure, as it implies that parties outside the employee group authorized to use the system will have to understand and work on the controls for the systems. These controls in the operating system include the logical security features. Therefore, the systems maintenance activities may provide a miscreant the potential for bypassing security controls through manipulation of operating system software or hardware.

Protection in this circumstance is extremely difficult to provide with any certainty. Office systems users should make sure that service people have signed nondisclosure agreements, and that people who work on systems are properly identified before the fact by their employer. In-house service people should be selected for their stability and reliability as well as for technical knowledge. Easier said than done! All maintenance actions should be documented and the reasons for the work well understood by responsible managers. Unannounced maintenance should never be allowed.

Expansion of the Trusted Group.   This concern is directly related to the one above, as the requirement for servicing of electronic systems implies an enlargement of the usual trusted circle. For any piece of information, the originator has some finite audience in mind. Whether an executive memo, a note to your husband or wife, a Greek-language newspaper in New York City, or a whispered aside to a trusted associate, the originator has a limited information distribution intended. In physical or oral information passing, restriction of the audience is fairly simple. The weaknesses of the human memory are an effective limitation on orally passed information. Think of how often people use the term "I believe" when making a statement! Paper-based information can be controlled through the use of handwritten notes, sealed envelopes, registered mail, etc., although the copier has certainly put a chink in that armor!

Electronic information, especially with regard to interconnected office systems, is another matter. Information can be at two points thousands of miles apart, almost simultaneously. Ineffective control systems or system failures can result in misrouting of information with embarrassing results. Several cases are known where payroll information appeared unbidden and unwanted at distant printers in foreign businesses. Cases of "ghost" or stray data circulating through networks are not uncommon.

Intentional or chance penetrations through manipulation of the system during maintenance of hardware or software is not unlikely. Consider the case where a defect in a magnetic medium (tape or disk) requires the maintenance person to attempt retrieval of information. This is an evident case where the information will be exposed to an outsider in the course of authorized activity.

There are many circumstance wherein unauthorized activity, perhaps in conjunction with routine servicing, could result in information exposures. Since office information tends to be in more finished form, the penetrator gets more for his (or her) effort if the target is well planned.

Another aspect of the vulnerabilities resulting from an enlargement of the trusted circle and system software involves the concept of "distributed computing." Originally, computers operated at only one location. Then terminals allowed connection to distant points, where users could share the computing power. Each computer, however, had a unique operating system, with varying features which made interconnect and data interchange difficult or impossible. Distributed computing means that a series of interconnected computers share the same executive or operating system, thus being able to exchange information and services as though many were one. This also means that operating systems changes, and hence changes to security controls, may potentially be made to all units from a distant station. Good procedures and administrative controls for systems changes and user recognition of such changes are important to maintain system integrity.

Some distributed office systems use coaxial cable as a sort of "data pipe," transmitting all messages or information to all stations. The correct station (as addressee) sorts out the messages intended by examining the addressee codes and rejecting those messages for other stations. If a station can be clandestinely attached to this cable, the potential exists for copying off all traffic and examining same at leisure. Cables should therefore be protected the same as any other hardware. They should not go outside control of the using business. Where connections are made to public utility lines, encryption is the security solution.

Management Control Over the Information Resource

Personal computing, as implemented in office automation, distributed computing, intelligent work stations, and other new applications of computing technology, is happening because of continuing, substantial reductions in the cost of computing. Since management control over a resource generally relies on approvals of procurements above some specified cost level, the availability of cheap computing means that information processing resource control is slipping away from management. To put it in other words, management control does not generally extend to purchases and use of pencils and paper — these are items whose costs are too low to justify case-by-case approvals in a large business. Similarly, calculators, typewriters, and other items may be purchased out of "local supplies" budgets by office managers. The decreasing costs of computer equipment, especially costs of personal computers, are now so low that these items often fall within discretionary procurement approval limits. Hence, management control of the information processing resource, once ironclad due to the high cost of big, central computers, is deteriorating.

More than mere control of expenditures is at stake. Big-business managers are recognizing that information is a key resource. Many large companies have "information management" vice presidents or directors. Control of the information resource is, in large part, the same as control of the information processing and communicating (network) environments. An important element in such management is security, which depends on information valuation and knowledge and control of the information sources, processing units, paths, and connections. The low cost of the new office automation technologies calls into question businesses' traditional means of control, the requirement for authorization for spending!

Effective electronic information security programs are one answer to this problem. An effective information valuation and protection effort places responsibility for protecting the information resource with the information users. In such a situation, management's inability to control the growth of the information network and its processing nodes becomes less threatening.

DATA PROCESSING AND TELECOMMUNICATIONS OPERATIONS

While a data center is different in mission and scope from a telecommunications center, both have computers and both process information. In some cases, the similarities outweigh the differences, especially where large data traffic network switches are in operation. In these environments, the responsible management must deal with electronic security in two modes. First, access to data via the physical facilities of the data center or telecommunications center must be controlled. That is, access to information on tapes, disks, or cartridges, and access via terminals of other connection devices internal to the data center must be strictly and severely controlled. Usually this means that, in addition to the usual controls over physical entry to the plant, certain areas inside the building must be further restricted. These usually include the operations area (where consoles are located), disk, tape, and cartridge storage and use areas, output processing areas (paper and microforms), and communications equipment rooms. Second, logical access control resources must be provided on a "menu" basis to the customers of the data processing and telecommunication service activities. These should consist of:

1. Additional restrictions on the handling or processing of information with a value factor assigned, available as optional steps when required by the customer;
2. Logical security subsystems (e.g., file, record, or data element passwording capabilities), which may be selected and applied at the discretion of the user;
3. Encryption systems, implemented as hardware or software, for use when information sensitivity dictates.

A most important observation here: the data center or telecommunications manager provides some standard level of security to meet routine needs. Incremental security elements, applied for high value factor information at user request, are the responsibility of the functional manager using the data processing or telecommunications service (and may be paid for by that manager).

For a long time, business people looked to the data processing manager to make security decisions on information processed and to implement those decisions within the area of responsibility. This begs the question of the security of that same information in hardcopy form outside the data center. Real security for information requires a recognition and acceptance of responsibility by the originator and functional users of the information. The data processing and telecommunications functions are service activities and cannot be expected to generate decisions concerning information sensitivity. Effective protection for information occurs only when management (user?) demands the necessary security from the data processing/telecommunications activities and from direct information users outside those areas.

The Menu.   By establishing a standard set of security features, the information processing operations can limit the variety of security measures required and requested. A listing of these offerings, published for the users in a menu format, encourages their use and establishes a justification requirement should additional or different protection be requested.

Physical Offerings.   *Input processing:* all batches can be processed and moved with covers, and receipted at each step. *Output processing:* printers and micromation units can be segregated by means of screens or restricted areas during the processing of certain runs. Reports can be stamped, overprinted, specially covered, numbered, packaged, etc., so as to provide positive control and limit exposure. Generally, these measures would tie into established company policies regarding marking and handling of high value factor information.

Logical Offerings. These subsystems, usually appended to or part of the operating system, allow various levels of access control, at the option of the user. Examples are the IBM RAC-F package, the Cambridge Systems ACF-2, and the Honeywell Multics operating system features.

A user or data owner may choose to have files "public," at one end of the security spectrum, or to establish controls down to the data element level. Generally, the more recent software packages offer increasing flexibility and protection. ACF-2, for example, is a very powerful protection tool (the effectiveness of any package depends on the user's willingness to apply it properly).

Each data processing center should have a security coordinator with suitable skills to control and monitor the security subsystem and its environment. Generally, the tasks consist of interface with the systems maintenance activity and with the data processing users. The user management must indicate (preferably in writing to ensure accountability) those access authorizations needed for business purposes. The data processing security coordinator and staff then make user-authorized changes to access authorization tables in the security subsystem. This activity includes installation and maintenance of the security subsystem's software, often with some vendor assistance. There may be a significant workload in the effort. A large corporate data center may require four to five people on the security staff.

Eventually, and probably within the next five years, the implementing of access management decisions will move to the user's office. Today a decision to restrict access is usually conveyed by word of mouth or memo to the data center, where a security coordinator makes the changes. This activity is fast becoming too much to handle, as hundreds of decisions must be implemented. Modern access management systems will allow the functional user to make access authorization changes directly, via a terminal, to the security subsystem. This of course finally recognizes the point made above; that is, that the data center or telecommunications manager is only responding to user security requirements.

Telecommunications Risk Environments

Many security exposures exist in telecommunications systems and applications. In any modern, worldwide company, all time-sensitive information is transmitted electronically. Such transmissions offer tempting targets to industrial espionage agents and, more importantly, are susceptible to those elements of society intent on mischief. In this group are employees seeking satisfaction or profit, groups with political ends, and organized crime.

Business vulnerabilities fall into two general areas. The most severe risk is that of the loss of information integrity, privacy, or availability due to actions of employees. A second and lesser risk is from exposure of information to damage or destruction because of the acts of outsiders. Both areas of vulnerability occur in these risk environments: (1) the environment wherein information form is changed and (2) the environment in which information is in transmission.

Risk Environment 1 — Change of Form.   Information changes form when it is converted from human-use format to machine-use format. For example, human voice is changed to analog signal when one speaks into a telephone or feeds paper into a facsimile transmitter. A form change also occurs when data are transcribed from paper to a keyboard-initiated signal or from a scanned printed format to electronic signals. The result of all this activity is, similarly, a change of form, which is called output.

In this risk environment, security is usually compromised because of eavesdropping (unauthorized listening) or because of unauthorized observation. In essence, this risk environment calls for proper physical protections (door locks, restricted areas, screening) and good procedure (do not discuss classified information on the telephone in a public place; keep documents covered; restrict access to documents).

Risk environment 1 is not a case for technical security measures, except in the rare instance where shielding to prevent emission pickup from conversations might be desirable. This is a general case (see Recommended Readings, Appendix 1) and not directly related to telecommunications.

Risk Environment 2 — Information Transmission.   Information is in transmission continually, in electronic form, via hardware or radio (microwave) circuits. Included in these circuits are switching centers and junction boxes. Circuits carrying information travel through physical areas which must be considered hostile. They are outside the control of the business user. They are also subject to simple, easy, and relatively cheap interception. Information-carrying circuits include public telephone lines and microwave links. Both may be tapped or intercepted. Traffic may be recorded and analyzed in depth, at leisure, and such activity requires only a modest investment in terms of potential values.

Telephone and data link switching centers and connection boxes offer simple, easy-to-access physical connection points for temporary and long-term eavesdropping or copying of voice and data traffic. Many of these physical elements are outside the control of the using business, and even those within a company's facilities are often poorly protected. In most cases, these elements are maintained by the employees of other companies, and so offer tempting targets for would-be intelligence gatherers.

Security Measures

In all cases of vulnerability described, primary security rests with effective protection of facilities. That is, effective management and restrictions of access to, and operation on, communications facilities under business user control, and good procedure on handling information at change-of-form locations. Secondary protection, that which would safeguard information in transmission, requires data transformation or encryption of traffic. That is, all high value factor communications traffic, including voice and facsimile, must be transformed using an encryption algorithm. This may be accomplished through installed hard-wired hardware, software, or hand-held partial-message encryption devices. The four levels of security apply.

Before such measures for technical protection can be used, certain prerequisites must be met:

1. Technology must be available to make the protection reasonable and cost-efficient in the business situation.
2. Managers using the telecommunications facilities must believe that the risk exists, and that it justifies the effort of protection.

Encryption technology is fast developing and is available today to cover all the risks, except in a few cases (e.g., dial-up time-sharing). But current technology is expensive and detracts from the convenience usually expected by users (see earlier discussion of encryption element).

Voice-encryption hardware is expensive but is now fairly convenient to use. Convenience and ease of use are directly related to cost. Hand-encryption devices (word encryptors) are inconvenient but relatively cheap and portable.

Current software products have high overhead costs. Hardware is effective only on a link basis, but is fast becoming economical.

Acceptance of the risk and need for protection is fairly low. Most managers do not really believe that their communications are seriously exposed. However, cases of telecommunications interceptions for purposes of crime or mischief demonstrate that encrypting links carrying volumes of sensitive traffic can pose a major security problem. The training of employees in awareness of voice communications exposures should be mandatory.

TIME-SHARING AND DISTRIBUTED COMPUTING

Time-sharing and distributed computing are closely related manifestations of one phenomenon. That is, people want to have computing power close to their personal business activities whenever it will help do the job. Time-sharing refers to the connection of multiple terminals to a central processor, where the speed and capacity of the central computer make the service to each user appear to be immediate. Distributed computing has the same effect, except that in this case each individual user has a processor which may or may not be connected to a central computer, but which is always connected to a network joining several similar units.

Important characteristics of time-sharing and distributed computing for electronic information security are:

1. Protection must rely on logical security methods, using hardware or software implementations, since these modes deliver computing power to many and remote locations (especially severe vulnerabilities in the case of "dial-up" services.

2. Personal identification is difficult and costly, since physical presence at an identity checkpoint is not practical. The systems must rely on password identification or "handshake" identification/authentication (when question-and-answer methods are applied).

3. Security depends heavily on individual system users accepting and complying with good security practices (e.g., keeping passwords private).

4. Since files may be created outside established structures (e.g., as with individuals using APL programming), access to supposedly private files may be gained through file design flaws or through failure of creator or user to apply protective features.

The security coordinator serving a population of time-sharing or distributed computing users has a large task in employee education and motivation. Since good policy and standards will require the data center or computing system designer to offer security alternatives, protection ultimately depends upon the personal acceptance of security responsibility by every user of the system. The security coordinator, in this case, may also be called upon to offer advice in setting up files and access control methods for time-sharing users. To do this, a competence in time-sharing technology in addition to a good grasp of security methods is needed.

Logical Security in Time-sharing/Distributed Computing

Logical security elements are those which permit the identification and authentication of a user, followed by his authorization to do certain preordained things (see a file, execute a program, modify a data element, etc.). In the traditional case, the logical security elements are supported and complemented by physical security elements. For example, the employee must gain access to the building and to the terminal room before "signing on." In the time-sharing/distributed computing situation, however, the user may be thousands of miles away. Logical security must then take up the slack in control caused by the inability of the security system to provide a physical check.

Various methods are available. Current technology is developing prototype hand geometry measurement devices and voice recognition systems. More commonplace are the ubiquitous passwords which for any degree of robustness must be combined with an authentication. This may be done by the user's providing an answer to one of a series of preset questions (e.g., what is your mother-in-law's maiden name?) or by requiring the entry of a date-related data item which, with the password, combines to form a valid authentication.

The third protective element of the logical security blanket is authorization. This means that, once identification and authentication are successfully completed, the user is limited through computer reference to a table (or similar method), to certain functions or files. Obviously, this not only limits what the authorized user may do, but it restricts the potential damage from a successful penetrator to only one portion of the data files.

Systems with only one of the three logical security elements are commonplace, but sadly undependable. The security coordinator must understand the exposures and be prepared to recommend reasonable implementations of measures which fit the sensitivity or value factor of the data.

In the early stages of the electronic information security program, a large expenditure of manpower and funds may be anticipated in the area of time-sharing and distributed computing. Most of this will be for the development and administration of logical security elements.

PROGRAM THEORY SUMMARY

The three-dimensional matrix (Figure 3.1) illustrates the program theory. In essence, the suggested electronic information security program is based on well-defined structure; business-wide applicability across all functions; effective protection through security elements applied in concentric levels, according to information valuation. The three-dimensional matrix can be used to view the program concept as a series of management actions. Each intersect of the three planes represents a directive and a set of reactions. For example, consider the intersect of the planes of executive program direction, office automation, and logical protection. Executive program direction is policy which may state that information is limited to those employees having a need to know. Office automation is a fairly unstructured environment typically using some form of distributed computing. Logical protection includes the security elements required for access management (personal identification, authentication, and authorization) and encryption.

At this intersect, executive program direction or policy should establish the requirement for protection of information at each of the potential valuations (e.g., registered, private, employee confidential, or similar). The policy must accommodate an environment such as office automation. It probably does this through general statements. Appropriate logical protection elements for the office situation must be described in a standard (another plane). The policy establishes the need for such a standard, so the reaction to the directive at this intersect is development of a standard for office automation.

At other intersections of the matrix planes, similar actions can be postulated. Actual implementation of the program is more direct, as the development and publication of policy, standards, and procedures provide an action framework. The evolution of the framework for a particular business is the natural result of a series of processes, called the program. The following sections and chapters outline these processes, in the rough sequence of actual occurrence, although some overlap necessarily happens.

The potential threat to digital electronic information is widely dispersed over a large, diverse population. Would-be penetrators may be attacking from varied environments, using many different systems and without regard to physical location or distance. The traditional security program, addressing the data center as the locus for concern, will not suffice. The security program for the 1980s must have

1. catholicity — the program must address all the various applications and circumstances of computer system use in the business; and
2. flexibility — the program must provide for reasonable management decisions in light of business requirements, while offering some generally acceptable level of protection.

The electronic information security program suggested by the matrix in Figure 3.1 provides a flexible, encompassing program with a dynamic management control process. This is a program attuned to the 1980s business environment.

4

GETTING STARTED

An established policy is the foundation for the electronic information security program. The next step is to develop detailed policy implementation requirements which are reasonably applicable across the company.

The corporate manager of electronic security and the unit security coordinators share responsibility for developing policy requirements. For our purposes we will call these "standards." Standards are the second level in the three-level policy structure shown in the three-dimensional matrix in Figure 3.1.

The corporate manager and the unit security coordinators form a committee, which uses the published policy and their knowledge and skills to research and build the set of implementing measures or standards. A set of such standards is provided in Exhibit 3.3, and forms the guidelines for operating unit action to meet policy intent.

The first draft, or the earliest agreed form, of the standards should be used by the security coordinators to perform a unit security requirements survey, described in the following pages. This survey allows management a look at the effort and cost which will be involved. Planning and budgeting for one or more years, in terms of what effort will be required to meet the policy, follows from the requirements survey. The survey will provide detailed information about the circumstances in each operating unit, thus serving as a good "sounding board" for further review and evaluation of the standard.

Within a reasonable time of publication of the first draft of the standard, and somewhat concurrent with completion of the requirements survey, the final, authoritative standard should be published. The standards then become the "target" for program actions; the requirements survey tools may be used again periodically as a security review method.

THE SECURITY REQUIREMENTS SURVEY

This "Requirement Survey" is based upon the newly published Standards for Electronic Information Security. The survey is conducted by the unit security coordinators. The approach, method, and effort to be put into the requirements survey depend on the nature of the unit being surveyed. Since the outcome of the survey will form the basis for planning program-implementing actions, the survey must be in enough detail to allow credible planning activities. A sample survey is provided as Exhibit 4.1, at the end of this chapter.

In a large technological organization, such a survey may require six months' time. An engineering group would be typical, where many computers are used and where unique circumstances, such as computer laboratories, may require special consideration. Comparatively, a marketing organization, operating through local sales offices, might be able to base the security requirements survey entirely on the headquarters and one typical branch.

These variations accent the importance of the unit security coordinator, with his or her familiarity with unit operations. In one actual case, the unit security coordinators prepared a survey form, collected information, and then wrote a series of computer programs to summarize and analyze survey data. This unit, it was discovered, had over a thousand computers in use! The process of conducting the security requirements survey in an operating unit may follow various paths, but generally the activities may be broken down into four phases.

Phase 1

The unit security coordinator will have participated in the development of the electronic information security standards. It may be assumed that the standards are relevant to the unit and its operating mode. In Phase 1, the security coordinator considers the application of the standards to the operating unit. Some portions may be considered to be fully accomplished; physical security in data centers is usually such an item. Other requirements may need further development or explanation, prior to conducting the survey. Such an item might be encryption, as most businesses are not yet involved in its use.

During Phase 1, then, the security coordinator develops a survey rationale suitable to the various security elements and their current status in his unit. The survey rationale may include such subject categories as:

- Fully accomplished, requirements survey not needed, coordinator can evaluate situation personally.
- Partially in place, survey need only ask appropriate question.
- Not widely understood, concept introduction required as presurvey.

- New item to unit, training required before survey respondents can reply intelligently.

Phase 2

The security coordinator should now be ready to prepare the survey vehicle. This may be a report to be prepared directly by the security coordinator, a personal survey based on visits to appropriate people and places, a mailed questionnaire, or any combination of these. Unit size, geographical dispersion of activities, technological complexity and diversity, and unit organization structure will bear on the survey vehicle selection. Exhibit 4.1 illustrates a detailed requirements survey form, designed for a specific application — the reader should modify to fit needs.

The use of a survey form is recommended. Such a form, as a questionnaire or fill-in sheet, insures that all subjects are covered, and that a written record of the responses is developed. This will be important later on in the program when ongoing program management requires that accomplishments be tracked against requirements.

Phase 3

This phase is the actual survey itself. A cover memo from a senior unit manager should ask, "What must be done to bring the unit into compliance with the Electronic Information Security Standards?" It is important to keep this in mind as the survey progresses. The relative difficulty of cost associated with compliance should be noted as part of the survey process, but is not relevant to answering the question. In other words, do not allow respondents to answer questions by merely saying, "It is too expensive." The ability or willingness of management to pay for compliance is a part of the postsurvey process. The requirements survey must provide information upon which management can base decisions to invest or to take risks.

The security coordinator, in conducting the survey, should act as impartially and objectively as possible. Management support for the security requirements survey, as discussed previously, is essential. At a minimum, the survey should answer these questions for each security element stipulated by the Electronic Information Security Standard:

- What are the difficulties foreseen?
- Is the technology required available?
- What will the total cost be?
- What are the timing constraints which will delay compliance?

Phase 4

Once the information from the survey is collected, it must be assembled, collated, analyzed, and presented to unit management. The level of detail to be presented depends on local management practice, but sufficient understanding must be offered so that unit managers can intelligently present unit decisions to corporate executives.

The output from the requirements survey is the business plan. This plan identifies the existing shortfalls versus the Electronic Information Security Standards, and specifies the actions, resources, spending, and timing of the unit's proposed actions to meet the standards. In most cases, unit or division management will look to the security coordinator to propose a plan. It may be well for the security coordinator to review a draft of the plan proposed with the corporate manager of electronic security.

The business plan (regenerated per the organization's planning cycle) then represents a commitment to action. Annual security spending plans will be based, in part, on remaining or new compliance items. Chapter 5 discusses application of results of the security requirements survey.

RISK ANALYSIS

We have all heard about market research which indicated that there was no market for such-and-such; but when the determined entrepreneur brought the product to market anyhow, he made a million dollars. The same judgments must be applied to risk analysis. We would prefer to be able to present senior managers with economic values representing our business risk with and without an electronic information security program. To date, efforts to do so have been compromised by

- a lack of actual case data on which to base probability estimates, resulting in the use of "learned judgments" and raising serious questions as to validity;
- a tendency to overlook serious (unforeseen) risk and to emphasize lesser exposures, simply because the "crime technology" is so new;
- excessive costs to perform an effective risk analysis, if such is possible, may not appear justified by the reliability of the results;
- a tendency to address the form of information (computer form) rather than the asset itself (information in *any* form).

Computer information processing in an organization of any significant size is a complex and technical matter. Managers trying to determine what to do to insure some acceptable level of computing security are faced with a bewildering problem. The potential sources and types of attack on computing systems appear endless. Total protection is prohibitively expensive. The established security organization is not usually equipped (or chartered) to deal with the matter. What to do? A risk analysis may be called for. Many proposals for a highly structured probability-based risk analysis have been made. Software packages are for sale, and the U.S. Bureau of Standards has published a procedure.

For the large company, a business-wide, rigorous risk analysis using currently fashionable methods is probably impractical. This is true because the number of exposures and the number of information processes are too great to be handled by any method claiming precision. The popular risk analysis methods have serious flaws, addressed below, which compromise the credibility of the results and make the considerable cost of such analysis a dubious bargain (*Business Week*, April 20, 1981, estimated $250,000 for a risk analysis for a $1 billion company).

For limited situations, such as a case where management wishes to know whether to accept a risk — perhaps because protection appears too costly — risk analysis of a general or rigorous nature may be worthwhile. Such an application might be one which involves a single system, say an order entry system using terminals at sales branches. The present mathematics-based risk analysis methods are less likely to become bogged down in masses of information, thus making the "fatal flaws" more manageable.

Most of the risk analysis methods deal most effectively with what might be called "disasters" — that is, the risk of fire, flood, or other destruction of processing capabilities. These are not trivial, but are not the primary concern here, not being within the definition of electronic information security. Building safety is important to information security — if the building is destroyed by fire, the information is gone — but facility safety systems are a separate matter, if for no other reason than to keep the subject within reasonable scope. But see the discussion on Contingency Preparation in Chapter 6.

A general set of methods and procedures is applied by all the structured mathematics-based risk analysis methods studied. Certain differences occur — some are implemented through computer programs — but the approach is fairly standardized.

Since most rigorous risk analysis proposals envision an analysis for an entire organization (an approach which is invalid, in the author's opinion), a committee is set up. The committee provides a range of knowledge about the business systems, activities, facilities, processes, and methods which must be considered in the analysis. The committee might include the systems group, the functional user group, computer operations, facilities maintenance, etc. The committee applies its overall knowledge to the development of the data for the risk analysis (which is essentially an application of probability theory).

Next, the committee lists all the vulnerabilities occurring as the systems and information processes proceed in the course of business. The committee assigns risk values, in terms of dollars, pounds sterling, or whatever, to each potential vulnerability event.

Now, the committee must estimate the possibility, or probability, of each event occurring. (Since there could be thousands of items in each of these categories, this is not a small undertaking!)

The conclusion of the study is a process of multiplying risk values by probability factors, to get an exposure cost. This exposure cost, or decision value, is then used by management to decide when and where to spend on security. (Often it is used by security people to try to convince management to spend...the author prefers a different approach.)

Details of Risk Analysis

In a large corporation, with multiple divisions spread over wide geographic areas, the size of the risk analysis committee must be large. Probably the committee would consist of division or area subcommittees. The size of the task of identifying the individual vulnerability-causing business activities is mind-boggling. Consider one function, accounts receivable. A look at such a function shows that vulnerabilities occur (a) whenever information changes form, as from paper to digital, or is transmitted via communications circuits; (b) whenever information is moved interorganizationally or functionally, as when an order is processed from accounts receivable through to commissions files. The potential vulnerability points in such a system, in a large business, could be in the hundreds. Total vulnerability points in the operations of a large corporation could be in the tens of thousands.

The committee's task, then, is a huge one. Without knowledgeable, capable people, the committee cannot do its job. If knowledgeable, capable people are assigned, they will be tied up for a long time. The conclusion is that popular risk analysis methods are costly. The fatal flaws in the method should raise serious doubts as to the justification of that cost.

The popular mathematical methods of risk analysis, unless constrained severely in scope, have serious or fatal flaws. As discussed above under cost, the potential numbers of vulnerability points may be very large. The first fatal flaw arises from this fact. The fatal flaw is:

THERE IS HIGH PROBABILITY THAT THE COMMITTEE WILL OVERLOOK A SERIOUS VULNERABILITY

A security program tied to a committee's listing of required protection points, with the potential for omissions, cannot be considered an acceptable program. A general approach using information valuation is, in the author's opinion, preferable.

The second fatal flaw in risk analysis is in the development of probability. The insurance industry uses a mortality table or other actual experience records to develop estimates of risk. No such historical data are available to the risk analysis committee. The probability assigned to each vulnerability point, that is, the likelihood of a security breach occurring at that point, is arrived at by consensus of the committee members. Webster's New Collegiate Dictionary says this is a "guess," i.e., "forming an opinion from little or no evidence." Using this method, a vulnerability estimated as a million-to-one shot may occur three times in the next year, while a one-in-ten estimated probability may never occur. Thus the second fatal flaw:

THE PROBABILITY ESTIMATES' VALUE WILL RANGE FROM DUBIOUS TO WORTHLESS

A risk value must be developed for each potential vulnerability, i.e., should the payroll file be compromised; what will it cost us? Generally, current risk analysis methods recognize the fallibility of this estimation. A typical approach is to apply order-of-magnitude values, e.g., the risk is $1,000, $10,000, $100,000, $1,000,000, etc. The third fatal flaw is obvious:

THE VALUES ASSIGNED MAY BE IN ERROR BY AN ORDER OF MAGNITUDE

The data generated by the committee during the activities described are now used to compute decision base results. These results, in the form of dollar figures, are purported to represent the risk involved in a vulnerability point. Management will then make decisions on computing security investments based on these decision base values. The decision base value is computed as follows:

(value of event)   times   (probability of event) equals (decision base value)

or

$$Ve \times Pe = DBV.$$

A very large array of events and risk values should result from the committee's work. The fatal flaws noted call into question the completeness and value of the data. Consider the listing in terms of the fatal flaws.

value of event   probability of event
(may be in error by   ×   (at best dubious, at
an order of
magnitude)   worst pure guess)

equals: list of decision base values
(which has high risk of being
incomplete or overlooking a significant vulnerability)

A Honeywell-sponsored survey or users of risk analysis methods, discussed at the Privacy and Security Conference in April 1979 in Phoenix, showed that of approximately fifty companies trying risk analysis almost 90 percent of those who tried were dissatisfied with results. No wonder.

USING INFORMATION VALUATION AS A GUIDE

For years business has used physical security programs based on good police practices. People who have tried to justify a guard on a gate based on risk analysis have quickly found that it does not work. This is so because the incidence of physical penetration or damage is insufficient to build a case for justifying specific expenditures (e.g., why should we have a guard on the east gate — no troublemaker ever entered *there!*).

Security has been a concern of mankind since cave-dweller times. Reasonable management takes steps to protect assets. Business owners demand such steps, for reasons obvious and common. Medieval kings built moats and fortresses and used spies to protect against overt attack and covert threats. Analysis was not required — experience and common knowledge were sufficient.

Modern business does the same in many instances, providing locking facility doors, guards, fences, remote scan television monitors, and other systems which recognize the facts of a world which is not benign. These protective measures are considered "reasonable and justified," based on a perception of the operating environment. This perception is the result of actual experience, the news media, discussions, and the application of professional knowledge from the security managers.

A similar process can be used to develop, tailor, and justify investment in the protection of computer-processed information. The information values, developed as described in Chapter 1, are used to determine the protective elements required at various stages of processing (including human processing). A well-designed program, based on information values across the total processing environments (see Figure 2.1) is equally effective, and much more economical to implement, than a total program based on risk analysis methods. Chapter 3 discusses policy and points out that security, like other business decisions, involves risk-taking. Within the established policy framework, division or unit managements continually evaluate risk versus security costs. Figure 4.1 illustrates the curves associated with achieving various levels of security for digital information. (These curves are not mathematically accurate, but are merely illustrative.)

An electronic information security cover presenting an extremely high work factor, or level of protection, will have an equivalently high cost in terms of administrative or procedural difficulty. As increasing numbers of would-be penetrators are shut out, the security mechanism also will deny entry to some number of authorized employees. An example will demonstrate the point.

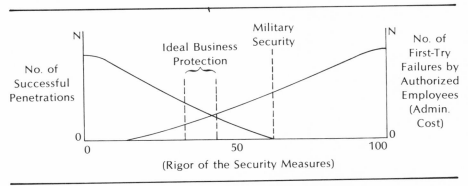

Figure 4.1. Relative penetration work factor (PWF) value *vs.* cost.

Assume that a data file, maintained on a magnetic disk device on-line to a terminal, has a password protection. The password is five positives long, and in fact is the name of the primary user of the file, "Nancy." Everyone in the department wishing to use the file may easily recall the password. And does. A penetrator, however, who has even rudimentary information about the business will know that Nancy is the primary system user, and will start off any penetration attempt by trying names associated with the primary user. Husband's, mother's, son's, and daughter's names are all good bets for discovery of a simple password. So, although the authorized employees find "Nancy" convenient, so will a reasonably clever penetrator!

Now let us assume that a program for electronic security is implemented, and the password is changed to a very rigorous form. That is, the password now is eight positions in length, and is randomly generated by the security subsystem. The password is now B933M12L. Not exactly the title of your favorite song. The penetrator faces an almost-impossible task. But the employees must continually call in the security officer, as they repeatedly forget or enter the wrong password. This administrative cost may be more than that justified by the additional security provided.

Security benefits, especially in the office environment, are extremely difficult to quantify. Management and the security staff must be continually aware of the necessary trade-offs, in terms of business operating requirements. Unrealistic security measures will be negated by the employees. In our example above, the employees would eventually write the password on pieces of paper, to be taped to terminal or wall. The security effect is then null.

Using information security management techniques as a basis for initiating a program of electronic information security has an important secondary benefit missing from the risk analysis method. That is, information must be protected in *all* forms, whether in computers, on paper, or passed by word of mouth. The total information security program should provide consistently effective protection across all forms.

A study of most so-called "computer crime" reveals that almost all cases begin with an exposure of information via paper — plain administrative carelessness. Locking up the computing systems without safeguarding the paper-borne information misses the point of computer security. The security effort must be a part of an overall information security program. After all, fraud occurred long before computers came on the scene.

SUMMARY

A detailed risk analysis is supposed to provide management with data upon which to base security spending decisions. The sparse supporting information and the analytical means available mean that decisions will be based on a large dose of "guesstimation," while exposures may be overlooked. Detailed risk analysis may provide management with a "security blanket" concerning spending and program thrust. Whether the cost of the analysis, which is significant if done properly, justifies this warm feeling remains to be seen. The security provided in comparison to that provided by using information valuation (Chapter 1), in the writer's opinion, does not justify the cost of formal analysis.

Risks are constantly shifting and changing in relation to technology developments. The use of judgment by skilled security people is the basis for both kinds of security program definition. Formal analysis generates the cost/risk trade-off data (of more or less dubious parentage) beloved of financial analysts. Management should choose the method which results in the greatest comfort — the results will probably be the same.

Exhibit 4.1. Security Requirements Survey

ELECTRONIC INFORMATION SECURITY REQUIREMENTS SURVEY

Budget Number_____ Preparer _____

Manager's Name _____ Date _____

Organization Name_____

INSTRUCTIONS

1. Assure that the information above is completed.

2. Review the remaining instructions and the questionnaire.

3. The manager is responsible for completing the first section for the entire business center. The last section may be delegated to subordinates.

4. A copy of the last section must be completed for each system/software application.

5. If a response of nonapplicable (N/A) is used, explain the reason why.

6. Please type or neatly print any narrative.

7. A copy of Corporate Policy is included.

NOTE: If you use no electronic information processing (computers, terminals, tele-copiers, word processors, printers) in your function, return this package with just the top of this page filled in.

ORGANIZATION AND ADMINISTRATION SECURITY

			YES	NO	N/A
POLICY	1.	Do you and your people understand the security requirements specified in Corporate policy?	___	___	___
NEW EMPLOYEE BRIEFINGS	2.	Are new employees performing digital information processing given thorough briefings on the policies, regulations, and practices of the organization with respect to information security?	___	___	___
USER RESPONSIBILITY	3.	Are systems users aware of their primary responsibility for the security of their information?	___	___	___

Exhibit 4.1.   Security Requirements Survey (continued)

			YES	NO	N/A
TECHNICAL SECURITY UNDERSTANDING	4.	Do data processing/systems/tele-communications people understand the information value factors?	___	___	___
SUPERVISION OF CRITICAL POSITIONS	5.	Do you provide effective supervision of employees in critical positions, and supervisory reaction to job performance problems which indicate potential security exposures?	___	___	___
JOB ROTATION	6.	Is it practice to rotate periodically those positions that have a potential for exposure?	___	___	___
JOB BACKUP	7.	Do you have backup (personnel, hardware, procedures) to perform all electronic information systems functions?	___	___	___
CONTINGENCY PLANNING	8.	Is there a current plan to assure operations during service interruptions or in case of disaster?	___	___	___
EMPLOYEE TERMINATION POLICY	9.	Are procedures in place to cause immediate restriction of a terminated/transferred employee's access to sensitive materials and areas including account numbers, passwords, and key cards?	___	___	___
ATTEMPTED VIOLATIONS	10.	Do you have a procedure to record and report any attempted violation of local security functions?	___	___	___
VENDOR/ CONTRACT SERVICES	11.	Is value factor information being processed in a vendor's computer, site, or with unique vendor software? If so,	___	___	___
		A. Has a nondisclosure agreement been signed?	___	___	___
		B. Has a risk analysis been conducted?	___	___	___
		C. Are there regular reviews and reporting of the vendor's security?	___	___	___

Exhibit 4.1.   Security Requirements Survey (continued)

		YES	NO	N/A
PHASE REVIEWS	12. Is security addressed during each phase review (initiation, definition, analysis, design, development, implementation) of any major system development project?	___	___	___
IRREGULARLY CHANGED PASSWORDS	13. Are passwords changed irregularly, but at least quarterly, upon termination or resignation of employees having had access to the combinations, or upon compromise?	___	___	___
COMPUTER INVENTORY CONTROLS	14. Is there inventory control of computer equipment, hardware, replacement parts, unused media, and supplies at all locations from arrival to end of useful life?	___	___	___
REMOVABLE STORAGE	15. Are there procedures and controls used in the management of removable machine-readable storage?	___	___	___
SHARED ACCOUNTS	16. Is the same computer account or access control used by more than one person?	___	___	___
KEY PERSONNEL DIRECTORY	17. Are names and telephone numbers of key personnel to be called in case of emergencies clearly posted in all critical areas?	___	___	___
SECURITY SUBSYSTEM ADMINISTRATION	18. Is there a formal assignment of security subsystem administration for systems processing classified data and all data base systems?	___	___	___
OVERALL SECURITY ADMINISTRATION	19. Is there a formal administration function for digital information?	___	___	___
	20. Is account usage and chargeback verified for each billing?	___	___	___
	21. Is an up-to-date list of all purchased and leased hardware and software maintained?	___	___	___

Exhibit 4.1. Security Requirements Survey (continued)

		YES	NO	N/A

PORTABLE   22. Is the use of portable computers or
COMPUTER/   terminals controlled via a sign-out log or
TERMINAL   assigned to an individual responsible for
                      knowing its whereabouts?   ___ ___ ___

CONFLICTING   23. Does anyone utilizing facilities/
RESPONSIBILITIES   equipment/supplies software, have con-
                      flicting responsibilities that contribute to
                      a security risk, e.g., report generation,
                      and report destruction and report
                      control; programmer, and computer
                      operator and operating system
                      maintenance?   ___ ___ ___

Level 1: Physical Security

DIGITAL INFORMATION PROCESSING DEVICE INVENTORY

Please complete for your function:

COMPUTERS

MANUFACTURER					
MODEL					
QUANTITY					

WORD PROCESSORS   REMOTE JOB ENTRY

Mfg./Model					Mfg./Model		
Quantity					Quantity		

TERMINALS/CRTS   PRINTERS   TRANSCEIVERS

Video	Hard Copy	*Low Speed	High Speed	Manual	Automatic

*Low speed is less than 120 characters per second.

Exhibit 4.1. Security Requirements Survey (continued)

		YES	NO	N/A

The following questions relate to access controls:

ACCESS CONTROLS 24. Do you restrict and control access to computing facilities? ____ ____ ____

MONITORING PERSONNEL 25. Is monitoring conducted for non-operational personnel who are permitted access? ____ ____ ____

ACCESS CODES 26. Are access codes changed regularly for digital access facilities? ____ ____ ____

SECONDARY ACCESS 27. Is there access to any controlled area from a secondary point such as service doors, windows, etc.? ____ ____ ____

Complete this section if value factor data is processed:

CLASSIFIED DATA 28. Is classified data processed? If no, go on to Question 37. ____ ____ ____

UNAUTHORIZED ACCESS 29. Are devices which are utilized to access/process value factor information located in an access controlled area? ____ ____ ____

VISITOR CONTROL 30. Are visitors to individual areas processing value factor data identified and logged upon entrance and exit? ____ ____ ____

PROPER IDENTIFICATION/ AUTHORIZATION 31. Is positive identification and authorization required for entering controlled areas of a facility processing value factor information. ____ ____ ____

LATENT IMPRESSIONS 32. Do latent impressions remain to be picked up after processing? (e.g., type-writer ribbons, etc.) ____ ____ ____

SANITIZING/ ERASING MACHINE-READABLE MEDIA 33. Are procedures for sanitizing/erasing classified media enforced? ____ ____ ____

WASTE CONTAINERS 34. Are containers readily available for disposal of classified waste materials? ____ ____ ____

LOCKABLE STORAGE 35. Is lockable storage used for value factor data? ____ ____ ____

SECURE AREA 36. Is high value factor data processed only on computers/terminals in secure areas? ____ ____ ____

Exhibit 4.1.   Security Requirements Survey (continued)

		YES	NO	N/A

The remaining questions on this page pertain only to computer operations under your control.

COMPUTER
OPERATIONS

37. Does your function operate a computer?
If no, go on to question number 44.   ____ ____ ____

SECURITY
FEATURE
AVAILABILITY

38. Do you provide, upon request, a description of available security features for users/system designers/programmers?   ____ ____ ____

VARIETY OF
SECURITY
FEATURES

39. Do you provide for all computers a variety of protective features which include suitable elements from each of the following categories:
A. LEVEL 1 — Physical Security?   ____ ____ ____

B. LEVEL II — Organizational and procedural security?   ____ ____ ____
C. LEVEL III — Hardware and software security elements?   ____ ____ ____
D. LEVEL IV — Encryption?   ____ ____ ____

STORAGE MEDIA
DEVICES

40. Do operators and users of devices creating information storage media apply a combination of protective measures which:
A. Positively protect and control all such media?   ____ ____ ____
B. Prevent the release of media containing information to any individual, unless specifically authorized?   ____ ____ ____
C. Insure that any shipment or transfer of such media between locations is via courier, insured express, sealed mail, or equivalent?   ____ ____ ____
D. When media containing value factor information is moved between locations, is the value factor clearly marked on the media container or reel?   ____ ____ ____
E. Are formal records maintained of the status, location, and disposition of each such medium?   ____ ____ ____

Exhibit 4.1. Security Requirements Survey (continued)

		YES	NO	N/A
DATA CENTER SUPERVISION	41. Do you provide active supervision of all activities, including positive management control over, and prior approval of:			
	A. All operating system maintenance actions?	___	___	___
	B. All hardware maintenance actions?	___	___	___
	C. All initial processor loading?	___	___	___
	D. All setting of system clocks?	___	___	___
	E. All changes to operating documentation, e.g., runbooks, job tickets, processing instructions, etc.?	___	___	___
DISASTER AVOIDANCE	42. Are facilities, both central and remote, constructed to provide the minimum level of protection as specified in policy against natural disasters and against persons intent on destroying property?	___	___	___
SYSTEM/ CONSOLE LOGS	43. Is a system log, console log, etc., sequentially numbered or otherwise controlled to insure a complete and auditable review of all actions?	___	___	___

44. If you have any further questions or comments on the first two sections (LEVEL II and LEVEL I), please provide them below:

_____

_____

_____

_____

_____

	Labor Hours	Expense	Capital
45. Provide an estimate of the number of hours and additional expenses/capital required for your budget center to comply with the organizational and physical aspects of this questionnaire.	_____	_____	_____

Exhibit 4.1.   Security Requirements Survey (continued)

DATA SECURITY
(BY SYSTEM/SOFTWARE APPLICATION)

Application Name_____Preparer's Name_____

Acronym _____Telephone Ext._____

Description_____

_____

_____

_____

_____

_____

APPLICATION TYPE CODE	PROCESSING TYPE	DATA CENTER LOCATION_____
☐ FINANCE	☐ BATCH	D.P. EQUIPMENT USED_____
☐ RESEARCH	☐ ON-LINE	
☐ DESIGN	☐ REAL-TIME	MFG._____
☐ SIMULATION		MODEL_____
☐ DATA ACQUISITION		
☐ CONTROL		
☐ OTHER_____		
_____		

- -

Main Language	☐	Subsidiary Language	☐	Number of Programs	☐	Lines of Code	☐
Year System Was Installed	☐	Economic End-of-Life Forecast		Planned Replacement Year	☐	Estimated Replacement Costs $000	☐

- -

Exhibit 4.1. Security Requirements Survey (continued)

VALUE FACTOR:		YES	NO	N/A
USER ASSIGNED	1. Has the user assigned a value factor to all input documents, displays, reports, and procedures?	___	___	___
I.S. ASSIGNED CLASSIFICATIONS	2. Have the individuals involved with electronic information systems reflected the above value factor in the files, programs, and documentation?	___	___	___
I/O VOLUME COUNT COMPARISON	3. Are there procedures and software to ensure that users compare I/O volume against predicted requirements?	___	___	___
I/O DATA MOVEMENT CONTROLS	4. Are there transmittal documents to effect positive controls (such as trace-ability) over data being moved between user areas and the computer center?	___	___	___
PASSWORD PROTECTION CAPABILITY	5. Does the computer contain a password capability? If no, go on to Question 10.	___	___	___
PASSWORD PROTECTION SYSTEM	6. Is a comprehensive password protection system provided to include initiation, disbursement, storage, and change of password?	___	___	___
PASSWORD GENERATION	7. Are there procedures and software to ensure generation of passwords that are difficult to guess or determine programatically?	___	___	___
PASSWORD PRINT SUPPRESS	8. Are passwords inhibited from display when entered through a terminal?	___	___	___
PASSWORD CLASSIFICATION	9. Are passwords classified and protected the same as the highest value factor information shielded by that password?	___	___	___
PROGRAM CHANGE CONTROL LOG	10. Are there procedures and/or software to effect complete control over program changes, such as change logs?	___	___	___
APPLICATION SYSTEM TEST	11. Are specific procedures, software, and guidelines used to ensure thorough testing of application systems before operational status is acquired?	___	___	___

Exhibit 4.1.   Security Requirements Survey (continued)

		YES	NO	N/A
SYSTEM STANDARDS	12. Are there procedures and software to ensure that all systems use departmental accepted/published standards?	___	___	___
DATA ISOLATION CONTROLS	13. Are there procedures, software, and hardware to isolate test programs from production programs and test data from live data?	___	___	___
DATA INTEGRITY	14. Do effective control features insure data integrity (e.g., batch totals, control totals, etc.)?	___	___	___
SYSTEM SECURITY FEATURES	15. Are the system security features described fully in documentation and acceptable to the users for everyday practical application?	___	___	___
	16. Are there instructions for control of passwords, authorizations and other security functions?	___	___	___
ACCESS DENIED DELAY	17. Does the security system cause a delay to be introduced whenever an access attempt is denied?	___	___	___
PROGRAMMING CHANGES	18. Is there a management approval in place for authorization of all program changes?	___	___	___
SYSTEM DOCUMENTATION	19. Is the system fully documented?	___	___	___
	20. Is the documentation stored in a secure environment (not in an individual's desk)?	___	___	___
DOCUMENTATION CONTROLS	21. Are there procedures, software, and special facilities to control access to the system and application documentation?	___	___	___
IMPROPER LOG-ON CONTROLS	22. Are there procedures and software to detect repeated attempts to log-on?	___	___	___
PROCESSING TIME CONTROLS	23. Is there a check of actual time of use against expected time for the application?	___	___	___

Exhibit 4.1.   Security Requirements Survey (continued)

		YES	NO	N/A
TAPE/DISK/CARD MOVEMENT CONTROLS	24. Is there ensured control of removable media movement through the operations area? This includes a capability for traceability and accountability, basically a requirement for external labels on all media?	___	___	___
MODULAR DESIGN OF SYSTEMS	25. Is simple modular system design and structured programming used?	___	___	___

THE REMAINING QUESTIONS PERTAIN ONLY TO SYSTEMS PROCESSING OR CREATING VALUE FACTOR (V.F.) DATA

V.F. DATA	26. Do you process V.F. data? If no, go on to Question 44.	___	___	___
FORMS CONTROL	27. Is forms control used for V.F. reports at remote sites to require operator intervention before reports can be printed?	___	___	___
HANDLING CLASSIFIED DATA	28. Do systems which process or create V.F. information include procedures which issue proper identification, marking, and handling of classified information?	___	___	___
	29. Is the output securely wrapped?	___	___	___
CASUAL OBSERVATION PROTECTION	30. Are V.F. inputs and outputs protected from casual observation at all times?	___	___	___
MEDIA STORAGE CLASSIFICATIONS	31. Are color-coded labels affixed to all V.F. storage media moved between locations?	___	___	___
I/O SEGREGATION	32. Are V.F. input and output kept separate from non-V.F. data?	___	___	___
I/O DATA STORAGE	33. Do you provide lockable storage for V.F. data, programs and reports?	___	___	___
SENSITIVE FILE ACCESS LOG	34. Do you log all accesses by system programs or application programs to files designated as V.F.?	___	___	___
CLASSIFIED REPORT MARKING	35. Is each page of a V.F. batch report sequentially numbered?	___	___	___

Exhibit 4.1.   Security Requirements Survey (continued)

		YES	NO	N/A
	36. Is the last page so noted?	___	___	___
	37. Is each page, and front and back covers, stamped with V.F. symbol or marked through program-generated printing in the upper right-hand corner?	___	___	___
USE OF VENDORS	38. Is V.F. information processed in a vendor's computer, site, or with unique vendor software?	___	___	___
STORAGE PURGE	39. Is an overwrite/erase of all types of storage accomplished after use for V.F. processing?	___	___	___
HI-V.F. DATA	40. Do you process HI-V.F. data? If no, go on to Question 44.	___	___	___
REMOTE ENCRYPTION CAPABILITY	41. Do you provide encryption capability for storing and transmitting HI-V.F. data at remote data processing facilities?	___	___	___
ENCRYPTION FOR TRANSPORT	42. Are HI-V.F. data to be transported by a third party outside the computer facility encrypted?	___	___	___
COMMUNICATION ENCRYPTION	43. Is encryption provided for HI-V.F. data passing over communication lines?	___	___	___

44. If you have any further questions or comments, please provide them below:

_____

_____

_____

_____

	Labor Hours	Expense	Capital
45. Provide an estimate of the number of hours and additional expenses/capital required to update this application to achieve compliance per the questionnaire.	_____	_____	_____

Exhibit 4.1. Security Requirements Survey (continued)

DATA SENSITIVITY 46. Does the system contain any of the following or similar types of data? *Check those included.*

Long-range and contingency plans	_____	Product life plans and reports	_____
Major new ventures	_____	Program papers	_____
Acquisition or sale of business or properties	_____	Early and sensitive product/system specifications	_____
Major curtailment of operations or manpower reductions	_____	Competitive assessments and comparisons	_____
Business strategy or product technology letters and reports	_____	Strategic alternatives	_____
Position papers	_____	Major personnel or facility changes	_____
Future product design and developments	_____	Consolidated plans	_____
		Other (explain)_____	

Source: Carl Grovanz, Xerox Corporation.

5

WORKING THE PROGRAM

At this point it may be well to review the activities which have established the program for electronic information security. In sequence, these activities are:

1. Publication of policy — this action establishes corporate management's intent to commit continuing resources to the safeguarding of business information wherever it occurs.
2. A network of security coordinators in the operating divisions or units is established, for both implementation and maintenance purposes.
3. Standards are developed and published — the security coordinators jointly develop and publish standards which will provide detailed requirements for support of the policy intent. Standards are the references for the division or unit business managers. Local procedure, if necessary, is developed from the standards.
4. Requirements survey — this detailed survey, against the established standards, provides input for business planning. The requirements survey identifies the actions, resources, and spending needed to achieve compliance, over a period of time. Typically, this time span may be two to three years.
5. Unit plan — this plan commits unit or division management to achieving compliance with policy and standards. The unit plan sets resource and spending levels, and establishes milestones for completion of tasks leading to a level of security commensurate with the standards.

Ongoing program management will require some means for monitoring and evaluating unit performance against plans. This sixth activity, called key indicator reporting, allows unit and corporate managements to observe unit

performance against plan, and to "take the pulse" of the program effort on a
periodic basis. Table 5.1 illustrates the six activities in implementing a program
for electronic information security.

PROGRAM CYCLE

The working program for electronic information security has an orderly,
cyclical flow of events, beginning with the inital recognition and commitment
by top management expressed in a policy statement. The cycle of events, some
of which repeat at a fairly regular timing, allows the program to regenerate
and remain current with technology application.

Table 5.1
PROGRAM ACTIVITIES IN SEQUENCE

Sequence	Activity	Description	Continuity
1	Policy publication	Management decision to commit to program for digital information security	One-time. Policy revision as needed (five to ten years)
2	Program organization	Appointment of security manager and unit security analysts	Permanent appointments
3	Standards publication	Joint development and publication of detailed requirements for achieving digital information security	Reissue on a two-to-three year cycle, or as required
4	Requirements survey	Detailed survey at unit level to identify actions required to meet policy	One-time. Input to 6. Unit plan
5	Unit plan publication	Unit-developed multi-year plan for resources, spending, and compliance activity to meet standards requirements	Annual review and reissue. Basis for key indicator reporting
6	Key indicator reporting	Quarterly or other periodic reporting against unit plan	Quarterly review by unit management and corp. staff. Annual review by corp. management

The program activities are driven by business requirements, which may also be the prime driver for new applications of computing technology. The program then also stays reasonably effective in consonance with business needs. This is most important. The electronic information security program must be suited to business requirements, no more and no less. Regular reviews and replanning activities help ensure currency and appropriateness to the business environment, which in a big company are always changing.

A large company, with sales of $1 billion or more annually, probably has a program cycle of about three years. That is, a three-year cycle is about right to

1.   establish policy and commitment;
2.   perform requirements survey;
3.   develop plans and standards;
4.   install security measures;
5.   review standards against business needs;
6.   reevaluate (via survey if appropriate) situation;
7.   regenerate requirements through new standard (or policy);
8.   obtain recommitment and support;
9.   develop new plans.

Plans are based on the inital requirements survey, which measures current situations against the standards. Plans will probably extend over a period of years, although annual reissuance of the plan is in most cases appropriate to mesh with business planning and funding cycles. Unit business plans should include resource needs for electronic as well as other kinds of security. Electronic security plans resulting from the security requirements survey provide the targets and schedules of accomplishment which should move the unit or division toward full compliance with policy. Compliance with policy is achieved when the unit substantially meets all the minimum protection levels established in the standards. In cyclical fashion, each unit's business plan should build on the previous year's accomplishments, moving the unit toward complete satisfaction of the work items identified in the requirements survey.

Eventually, probably about three years after initial program start, some units may wish to review the situation of requirements, spending, and achievements. Another requirements survey, or a lesser security review, would be appropriate for this purpose. About every two or three years, or as changes occur which impact business methods or technology applications, both policy and standards should be reviewed for currency. Today's rate of change and increasing use of computing make such reviews absolutely necessary if the electronic information security program is to be effective. Figure 5.1 illustrates the program cycle, which will be different in cycle times and content for each business situation.

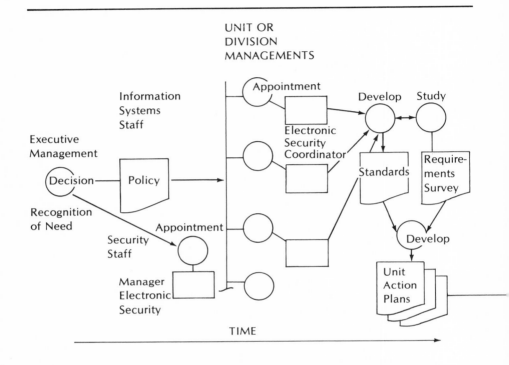

UNIT OR
DIVISION
MANAGEMENTS

Figure 5.1. Electronic information security program; program cycle and information flow.

REPORTING AND KEY INDICATORS

Regular evaluation of program progress, against established requirements, is accomplished via the reporting procedures. Evaluation of the effectiveness of applied security elements, as standards compliance is achieved, is another matter. This is a case of judgment, test, and analysis by competent technicians via security reviews or requirements surveys.

Corporate security staff should collect and assemble, for summarization for top management, data concerning "key indicators" which will provide information indicating the extent to which each unit or division is meeting plan requirements. It is well to accept the fact that perfect security is never achievable. Rather, security must be viewed as a continuum, with no security at one end and perfect security at the other. Although perfect security is never reached, the goal is continuing progress along the continuum in that direction.

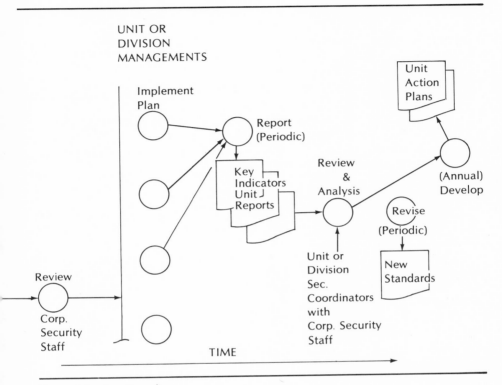

Figure 5.1. (continued)

The plan should provide such impetus. The key indicators should be selected so as to indicate to the security manager, and ultimately to top management, that orderly progress is being made at a satisfactory rate, i.e., per the plan. The key indicators have several functions:

1. they simplify reporting requirements for the units;
2. they simplify the task of the security staffs at all levels in evaluating progress against plan;
3. they indicate the important items versus the trivial;
4. they should allow cross-information about the progress of solutions aimed at common problems.

The security coordinator at each division or unit is the responsible action officer for insuring that plan schedules are accomplished. Although unit or division line management is ultimately responsible for security (this must have been established when initial policy was written), the security coordinator provides the managerial impetus to the program. The security coordinator does this by

1. working with line management to insure that appropriate funds are included in the unit budget according to the plan;
2. tracking progress against the plan and reporting this to unit or division management;
3. Reporting on key indicators to the unit management and to the corporate manager of electronic security.

The prime purpose for the security coordinator at each unit is cross-fertilization and the assignment of single points for resolution of common problems. The key indicators should provide a means for monitoring results and sharing benefits.

Examples of key indicators are given in Table 5.2. The corporate manager electronic security should develop those which best fit the program and plan requirements, along with any special interest items from top management.

Table 5.2 indicates that some activities have continuity, that is, they are more than one-time efforts. The key indicators established to monitor unit activity and progress are initiators for cyclical renewal of policy and standards. Unit security coordinators may identify new requirements or may find that already recognized security problems have novel characteristics requiring development of new security elements. Instances such as these should trigger an effort to revise or replace standards and, on a much longer term basis, may lead to rewriting of policy.

INFORMATION FLOW

The flow of information as to

*   requirements (standards) currency and acceptability;
*   newly recognized vulnerabilities;

Table 5.2
SUGGESTED KEY INDICATORS

Is year-to-date electronic information security spending according to plan?

Are all value factor files and systems protected by access management systems?

Is a formal security program established with specific assignments of responsibilities?

Are special interest development items proceeding according to agreed schedules?

- new or revised standards;
- problems and progress; and
- unit-developed procedure or method depends on the management relationships set up by the program. The security manager and the unit security coordinators together form a network for the transmission of information and assistance. The network also has a collective responsibility for the development of good standards. Line management direction flows from corporate management through the standards to unit or division management. In terms of directives, the security manager and the network are staff adjuncts, implementors, and reporters. Management operates and evaluates the program through the network.

Line Responsibility for Electronic Information Security

Functional users or originators of information are regarded as "data owners" for security purposes. To achieve full participation and, hence, effective security application by these information users, units may wish to set up management security councils. One appropriate reason for setting up a management review council or board in a large operating unit is to provide insight into new program directions. Information processing technology is among the prime driving forces for changes in the way business operates. As such, technology applications or intrusions into business practices almost always carry security implications. Were it possible to predict future requirements, an ongoing cyclical program would not be necessary. With technology development at its present rate, and projected to provide even more innovation in the near term, a unit information security review committee can help to keep the program effectively in perspective with business needs and methods. Members could include systems managers and functional managers, with a security coordinator or manager as recorder. Examples of situations where a management review committee fills a need are easily provided:

A personnel department wishes to have access to information currently in data files. A separate data base is set up, fed from the central files, and provided with inquiry capabilities. Who are allowed access, and under what circumstances? How will access controls be established and maintained? Are there various levels of access by job, salary, accessor responsibility, etc.? A review committee can assist in clarifying administrative positions which are essential to gaining control and insuring security for the information files.

A communicating word-processing and administrative services system is installed in executive offices. Who should have access? How are accessors to be controlled? Are there to be limits on the data stored or processed on the system? The management panel can get answers to these questions, and assist the security coordinator in implementing effective protection systems.

This need is not to be confused with formal risk evaluation (see Chapter 4, Risk Analysis). The security elements must be good enough to determine that risks and vulnerabilities are sufficiently offset. "Sufficiently" may be synonymous with "reasonably" since the security of computer-processed information must be provided for in a manner which harmonizes with overall business goal. The determination of what is "sufficient," or in harmony, is a continuing process. Inputs to the program cycle, in the form of recommendations from operating units, should flow through the unit or division security coordinators to the corporate level.

In the early years of program operation, comments will usually address additional coverages required. In later times people will begin to see overlapping coverages, redundancies, improved methods, and new technology which will allow some requirements to be set aside or replaced.

CONTINUING PROGRAM DEVELOPMENT

It is said that one never stands still, but either advances or slides back. A good program must have a continuing interchange of methods or ideas. The reader should not, in any case, consider the policy, standards, and security methods presented herein as gospel. Each business has its own characteristics and security requirements. Especially in the fast-developing application of distributed or "personal" computing, security requirements must be constantly developed and tailored to business needs.

To those ends, the program should offer some regular opportunities for key program participants to exchange ideas and to learn about new methods, from peers or experts. The idea of a "network" of security coordinators has already been mentioned. This group of knowledgeable people, from each division or unit, constitutes the most valuable resource in terms of contribution to program content and effectiveness. Some ideas on program development, especially where the business organization is a large one:

1. The corporate manager of electronic security could publish a regular newsletter on electronic security, providing ideas from the technical security literature, from peers at other companies, and from correspondents and, most importantly, telling what the operating units or divisions are doing. This could include plans, difficulties, and accomplishments.
2. Regular meetings of the division security coordinators, perhaps on a regional basis to conserve travel costs, could be held where these people could exchange ideas and contribute to mutual growth.
3. The corporation could sponsor a regular (annual?) electronic information security conference, with invited speakers on subjects of cur-

rent interest to the business. Often, computer vendors are happy to gain the exposure and can provide very capable technologists.

4. The corporate security director or staff should make periodic staff visits to the operating divisions. In some cases this may be for purposes of formal program status review, but at other times merely for a "hello" visit, perhaps with a helpful presentation on new program ideas or concerns.

A continual, information-rich exchange of ideas, needs, and solutions is an ingredient of a successful program. The many workshops, meetings, seminars, and conferences held by professional groups are excellent sources.

Training

The security coordinator is responsible for the training and currency of division personnel in the requirements of the security program. The standards are the basis for the training effort. For most companies, a formal training program, with copies of the materials being provided to each security coordinator, will be most economical and satisfactory in the long run. The goal is to achieve a common level of understanding and awareness throughout the company. Every employee using or processing digital information should have training.

A program based on announcements and the publication of materials will not succeed. Each employee must be indoctrinated with the importance of the security program. In the technical community, responsibilities for electronic information are greater, and training is especially important where people have personal computing capabilities. A good electronic information security program will provide

1. training materials suitable to all audiences;
2. electronic security awareness modules for inclusion in company technical training efforts;
3. pamphlets, hand-outs, and similar awareness builders;
4. periodic special security seminars (perhaps with the aid of computer manufacturers);
5. a regular newsletter or similar for those directly involved in computer security.

6

ASSURING PROGRAM VIABILITY

SECURITY REVIEWS

Management support, expressed through the commitment of resources, is the key to an effective electronic information security program. Unit or division managers, through the security coordinator, establish and maintain the required efforts. Periodic review of the unit or division security program is a good idea, however, because such a review provides a fresh view of the situation, helps create a cooperative effort among divisions and corporate headquarters, may identify problems which need to be addressed, may indicate the need for revision of electronic information security standards, and gives corporate management current information on the effectiveness and currency of division programs.

A security review is not an audit. Auditing (see following section) is a separate function which addresses the question of effective management control. A security review is a cooperative effort between corporate security staff and unit or division electronic security coordinators. The basis for a security review should be a checklist developed from the Electronic Information Security Standards. Such a checklist may be similar (though never the same) to the checklist used by the company auditors. Each important requirement from the standards should be rephrased as a question, preferably answerable by yes/no or satisfactory/unsatisfactory. The checklist should provide references to the standards with each question.

Since an electronic information security review is a cooperative effort, unit or division management must agree to, or ask for, such a review. Representatives of the corporate security manager and the unit security coordinator conduct the review. Unit management is given the opportunity to comment on the written report of the security review, before it is finalized. The agreed report should then be the basis for such action commitments as are appropriate. Actions required should become a part of the cyclical information security management process, described in Chapter 5.

Keep in mind that the review is never to be used as a basis for management criticism or punishment. It is a cooperative, constructive effort to understand the status of the information security program in the unit or division, and to develop suggestions for program improvement. Perfect information security is impossible to achieve. Do not be surprised or upset when deficiencies are noted in such a review. The goal is to continue to improve security in line with established policy requirements.

AUDITING

Although the network of security coordinators described earlier is the implementing means for a program for computer-processed information security, an enforcement mechanism is needed. People will do what they are supposed to do, and do it better, when someone is "checking up" on them.

The company auditors, or internal auditors, are the best enforcement means. While security and audit purposes do not always coincide, one overriding common purpose makes them good working partners. That purpose is the protection and conservation of company resources. Several benefits accrue from using the internal auditors to review security program compliance.

1. The auditors have an authoritative position which transcends local or division management.
2. Auditors are free from political entanglements, which may make difficulties for security staff.
3. Regular audits are scheduled for critical functions, thus giving management and security staff a chance for an objective review of the security effort.
4. Exchange of information between the audit staff and the security staff provides opportunities for general discussions of risks and concerns.

The security manager should establish working relationships with internal auditors and should prepare an audit checklist for the use of the auditors. They will probably revise the checklist to fit in with the particular audit style used in the company, but the input from the security manager will ensure that audits take security concerns into account and address the critical issues.

Computer-trained auditors are a necessity if such a liaison is to pay off. Suitable auditing software packages should be available. Auditors should go to their work equipped with the latest version of company security standards, and an understanding of the import of those standards. The security manager has a role to play in indoctrination of auditors on the intent and procedures of the company program for computer-processed information security.

Audit reports should always include a security module, one which addresses the security requirements for the particular function being audited. When computer systems or computing devices are in use at the audited function, the auditors should always make comment about whether the applicable standards are being followed.

The security manager should be provided a confidential copy of all draft audit reports. Comments on the audit work results can then be made to the audit coordinator or other official, who can see that proper corrective action is directed as part of the ongoing audit process.

An important side benefit from having auditors review security program compliance is that the security staff members remain insulated from an "inspection and audit" activity. This means that security "reviews" can be conducted with the full cooperation of division or regional staffs, in the knowledge that forthcoming reports will be recommendations and not directives. The cooperation and openness needed to ensure a good security program will not be compromised by fear of unfavorable reverberations through the lines of authority.

CONTINGENCY PREPARATION

In the author's view, contingency planning is a separate subject which addresses management's responsibility for broad planning for cases where protective systems fail or are overcome by nature or events. Because a limited contingency planning activity is usually associated with electronic information security, the subject will be discussed briefly.

Contingency planning cannot be done effectively if it is limited to a portion of the business. Making contingency plans for data processing while ignoring potential disasters in other, equally important parts of the business, is irresponsible. For one thing, distributed personal computing is moving the computer resource out into the organization, where the computing elements will be dispersed. A loss of a major office building could result in the loss of a significant computing resource, totally outside the data center.

The loss of a key manufacturing facility or the loss of a source of critical parts or supplies could be as crucial, or perhaps more so, to continued business operation as the loss of a data center, depending on the business.

Contingency planning is too important to be left to the information systems and security people. It must be addressed as a major corporate issue, on a broad, all-encompassing basis. Security and information systems managers have a role to play, but it must be within an overall business requirements framework to be effective.

All businesses should maintain programs of insurance and disaster planning which are complementary. As in the case of a personal insurance program, coverage should be limited to those risks which the business is unwilling to bear. An outline of a contingency program might include:

1. Loss of business insurance — deductible policy.
2. Recovery and alternative processing plans for those few information systems essential to the continued viability of the business, e.g., billing and receivables, payroll. It is doubtful if any large company can reasonably plan replacement of its system or network in total.
3. Recovery and alternatives planning for any key production elements, e.g., parts manufacturing.

Good security and safety planning and implementations should help avoid situations where the contingency plan must come into play. But note that contingency planning is a separate issue. Security programs, including that for electronic information security, are part of the management responsibilities for ongoing business operation. Contingency planning, on the other hand, is concerned with the possibility that ongoing operations may be halted because of circumstances beyond management control.

Contingency planning is strategic in nature; security planning is tactical. Contingency planning must therefore be done at the highest levels, and may involve decisions concerning elimination of major portions of the business or its assets. The contingency planning process might include:

1. Determine key activities for business continuity. These are the major production, marketing, and administrative functions which must, at any cost, be maintained if the business is to survive. This decision must be made by the chief executive or by a committee appointed by the CEO.
2. Identify the resources involved in those key activities. Some of those resources will undoubtedly be information systems.
3. Develop recovery and alternative operation plans for those resources supporting the key activities.
4. To the extent practicable, rehearse the implementation of the contingency operation, at least in simulated form. Be as realistic as possible, and keep scrupulous notes of activities and problems.
5. Continue to refine and improve contingency planning.

If thorough planning is difficult in the usual business environment, it will be even more difficult after the catastrophe has happened. The most difficult step is the first one. Each functional executive wants to see his activity as important to the business, but the company cannot plan to recover from every possibility. That is why the business insurance is provided. Only the very few, truly essential elements can be protected through contingency planning.

7
THE FUTURE

Rapid developments in computing hardware technology will continue to drive businesses, especially large ones, to automate functions previously performed manually.

- Hardware technology will provide smaller and more economical computing elements, almost as a reducing logarithmic function (cost and size reduced by 50 percent annually)
- Automation of functions will increase as the increasing cost of labor and decreasing cost of computing power provide a powerful economic driver
- The period 1980–1985 will see many new "pockets" of automation, especially in offices. These may be places where computing systems have a good "fit" to particular needs. General automation of business administrative and communications functions will not occur until later.
- Computing power will continue to increase spectacularly as instructions processed per second (MIPS) double with the introduction of each new technology.

From a security view, this implementation of computing systems in all phases of business operations implies greater movement of information in electronic form, and as a result, greater vulnerability to clandestine, unauthorized access. This exposure will be most severe where information mode (such as physical, on paper, and electronic, as in a computer) changes, usually involving human intervention. These mode changes will be most common, and the vulnerability of the information most serious, around the "pockets" of automation. These pockets will occur wherever office or administrative systems are converted to automated methods.

For example, a group of executive secretaries in a division headquarters may be provided with information processing systems which can handle text processing, communications, filing, "electronic mail," and graphics. Other secretaries in that division, however, and secretaries in other parts of the corporation may not have such equipment. The secretaries using the computer systems must then receive some information in paper form and must convert it to electronic form for the electronic mail and file system. Conversely, they will have to print out memos and letters, either locally or at remote stations, for delivery to those secretaries not having computer communications. This conversion process is a danger point.

Whenever the information exists in two forms at one time, there is increased risk. Additionally, as new systems are installed and new pockets of automation are created, there are temporary risks in each case until the old methods are phased out. These risks result from

1. the learning curve in coping with new requirements;
2. a tendency to revert to old methods if difficulties arise, therein possibly skipping security requirements;
3. the human tendency to have "backup" duplicates, just in case a new method does not work so well.

The prognostications for the continued deliveries of more advanced, faster information processing and communications services at the personal and organizational levels mean that the cyclical program regeneration process will be absolutely essential. This process, wherein policy and standards are renewed on a cyclical basis, is the only way to keep the electronic information security program abreast of technology. An effective program for electronic information security is not a luxury, but a necessity.

EPILOGUE

The approaches, strategies, and methods discussed in the previous chapters have been used in an actual business situation, a large multi-national. There were no well-defined guidelines when the assignment developed — ideas were generated through readings, discussions, and experience. The ideas for the program were then reviewed by management, put into place, and applied to the real business world.

How did things work out? For one thing, senior managers were most supportive. The requirements survey described in Chapter 4 developed a set of resource and spending targets, and actual investments have proven to be remarkably close to those targets over a period of years.

The unit security coordinators network has developed into a responsive and dedicated group of technologists. Regular meetings of the group have been a fertile source for exchanges of information, methods, strategies, and mutual support.

The basic program structure of policy/standards/procedures has held up and a program cycle of about three years has proven to be effective in staying abreast of applied computing in the business.

Is the program effective? This is a difficult question to answer definitively. The business does know that there are security exposures and that the program allows us to address these exposures. The security coordinator network provides more information about the real world than previously received. Evidence indicates that the electronic security program is a good investment and yields management and control benefits beyond basic security effects.

REFERENCES AND RECOMMENDED READING

REFERENCES

1. Martin, James. *Security, Accuracy, and Privacy in Computer Systems.* Englewood Cliffs, N.J.: Prentice-Hall, 1973, p. 400.
2. Cougar, Daniel. 1980 Xerox Information Management Conference.
3. Hosage, Markley, et al. "Data Communications/Office of the Future." *Telecommunications* 13 (September 1979), p. 58.
4. Mayo, John S. "VLSI." *Computerworld* 14 (June 23, 1980).
5. Hoffman, Lance. *Modern Methods for Computer Security and Privacy.* Englewood Cliffs, N.J.: Prentice-Hall, 1977, p. 11.
6. Hemphill, Charles, Jr., and Hemphill, John M. *Security Procedures for Computer Systems.* Homewood, Ill.: Dow Jones-Irwin, 1973, p. 111.
7. Hoffman.
8. Systems Development Corporation. "The Network Security Center — A System Level Approach to Computer Network Security." Washington, D.C.: National Bureau of Standards Special Pub 500–21, pp. 18-25.
9. Tuchman, W.L., and Meyer, C.H. "Efficacy of the Data Encryption Standard in Data Processing." New York: IBM Corp., 1978.
10. Needham, Roger M., and Schroeder, Michael D. Using Encryption for Authentication in Large Networks of Computer. Xerox Palo Alto Research Center, 1978.
11. Tuchman.
12. Kent, Stephen T. Protocol Design Considerations for Network Security, MIT Laboratory for Computer Science. NATO Advanced Studies Institute, September 1978.
13. Parker, Donn B.; Nycum, Susan; and Oura, S. Stephen. *Computer Abuse.* Menlo Park, Calif.: Stamford Research Institute, 1973.
14. Bequai, August. *Computer Crime.* Lexington, Mass.: Lexington Books, 1978, p. 4.

RECOMMENDED READING

Security Technology

A. Martin, James. *Security, Accuracy, and Privacy in Computer Systems.* Englewood Cliffs, N.J.: Prentice-Hall, 1973.

Reference 4, Hoffman, above.

General Discussion of the Subject

B. Kraus, Leonard I., and McGahan, Aileen. *Computer Fraud and Counter-measures.* Englewood Cliffs, N.J.: Prentice-Hall, 1979.

C. Katzen, Harry, Jr. *Computer Data Security.* New York: Van Nostrand Reinhold, 1973.

Risk Analysis

D. Courtney, Robert H. *Security Risk Assessment in Electronic Data Processing Systems.* New York: IBM Corp., 1978.

E. Reed, Susan K. *Automatic Data Processing Risk Assessment.* Washington, D.C.: National Bureau of Standards NBSIR 77–1228.

Encryption

References 6, SDC, and 7, Tuchman, above.

Legal Aspects

F. Bequai, August. *Computer Crime.* Lexington, Mass.: Lexington Books, 1978.

Information Classification

G. Post, Richard S., and Kingsbury, Arthur A. *Security Administration.* Springfield, Ill.: Charles C. Thomas, 1977.

Physical Security

H. Cole, Richard B. *Principles and Practices of Protection.* Springfield, Ill.: Charles C. Thomas, 1980.

INDEX

James A. Schweitzer, CDP, is Systems Technology Security Manager for Xerox Corporation, a major producer and marketer of office equipment. Prior to his current position, Mr. Schweitzer was Manager, Mail & Printing Systems Centers, and Manager, Commercial Data Center, for Xerox. Other experience includes consulting with the corporate systems staff at Dart & Kraft Corporation, and auditing for the U.S. Air Force Inspector General.

Mr. Schweitzer holds a M.B.A. degree from Indiana University, a B.S. in Management from Duquesne University, and a Certificate in Data Processing.